JAIL BIRD

The Life and Crimes of an Essex Bad Girl

TRACY MACKNESS AND DEBORAH CREWE

**SIMON &
SCHUSTER**

London · New York · Sydney · Toronto · New Delhi

A CBS COMPANY

First published in Great Britain by Simon & Schuster UK Ltd, 2013
A CBS COMPANY

1 3 5 7 9 10 8 6 4 2

Simon & Schuster UK Ltd
1st Floor
222 Gray's Inn Road
London WC1X 8HB

www.simonandschuster.co.uk

Simon & Schuster Australia, Sydney
Simon & Schuster India, New Delhi

A CIP catalogue record for this book
is available from the British Library.

This book is a faithful account of the author's experiences.
However, some names have been changed to
protect the privacy of certain individuals.

ISBN: 978-1-47110-090-1
Ebook ISBN: 978-1-47110-091-8

Typeset by M Rules
Printed and bound by CPI Group (UK) Ltd, Croydon, CR0 4YY

To Mash, Gravy, Sausage and Chops.
And Louie

CONTENTS

Prologue ix

1. Daddy's Little Princess 1

2. 'What are you going to do about it?' 21

3. Stella 35

4. Teenage Kicks 43

5. Gypsy Woman 59

6. Stir Crazy 67

7. The Only Way is Magaluf! 79

8. Girl About Town 89

9. They're Not Mine 109

10. Going Down 121

11. Banged Up 135

12. On the Out 147

13. Gangster's Moll 159

14. The Deal 173

15. The Trial   181

16. Big Bird   191

17. Biddy and Me   211

18. The Giggly Pig is Born   221

19. Tracy the Pig Farmer   233

20. Learning from the Past, Dreaming
    of the Future   251

    Acknowledgements   262

PROLOGUE

I'll never forget it – the moment I met Biddy. It was the turning point of my life, although I didn't know it then.

What I did know was that me and her, we had something
in common: we were both pissed off. She was pissed off
because that morning she'd had her babies taken from her.
They were ten weeks old and needed to be fattened up, ready
for slaughter. Me? I was pissed off for other reasons.

I'd been transferred that morning – a steaming hot day in
the middle of July. No one here knew me, no one respected
me. I didn't know the routine, I didn't know the people, I
didn't know what it was going to be like. I was back at the
bottom of the heap again.

They'd strip-searched me, and shown me my bed – the bed
in the horrible-est, tiniest, stuffiest corner of the biggest dorm.
Then they'd said I should see the farm. We set off down the
concrete driveway – me, my friend Louise, the only girl I
knew there, and Mr Coveney, the officer who ran the farm.

The farm was a bunch of sheds and huts about five

hundred yards from the main building. Beyond it was the most amazing view I had ever seen. Miles and miles of green fields, everything green. For years in the closed prisons all I'd done was look out of my window through bars at the building opposite. I couldn't enjoy the view over the fields though. I felt too apprehensive. I felt sick, on edge, like the first day at a new school. It was confusing, too, to be out in so much open space.

The first thing that hit me, before we even got to the farm, was the smell. It was horrendous. Like horse manure, but worse, and mixed with something musty and rotting. It was like the smell filled up my whole mouth and nose and I couldn't breathe. It was a shock to the system; it was too much. I gagged.

My mantra to get me through every difficult thing had become 'Deal with it'. Some days I would have to say it to myself over and over: 'Deal with it, deal with it, deal with it.' But I didn't think I could deal with this. I wanted to turn around and walk away.

We got a bit nearer and I saw the girls working there. I was careful not to catch anyone's eye but I knew without looking that they'd all stopped what they were doing to silently watch me. They had tied the top halves of their green overalls round their waists, and they had little skimpy tops on underneath. One girl had cut off her overall trousers so she had shorts on over her thick prison socks and work boots. A couple were on tractors with trailers attached. They all looked brown, and fit, and sweaty.

My mind started whirring away. I was doing the calcula-tions quick as I could, trying to spin out the walk down the driveway to give myself time. I thought, it smells of shit and worse, but you're out in the sun, getting a tan, keeping fit, you might get to drive a tractor. So I didn't turn around, I kept on going.

We got to the farm, and they took me to the pens. It was what they call a dry sow yard, with about ten pens in it. In each pen was a massive sow, and each sow had loads of babies. Most of the sows were just lying there on their sides, not moving, with the babies all on them, getting milk. That was quite sweet. In one pen there was an enormous boar. The smell here was worse, if that was possible. Now I was closer to the shit and the silage – and there was the over-powering fusty smell of damp animal mixed in too. There were flies everywhere, and a board up with names and num-bers written on it – Babble, Rosie, Dictator, 2 kg, 3 kg, 14 x 1 kg. It didn't make any sense to me.

It was a big shock. I hadn't thought about any of this when I'd filled in my form – the smell of them, and the size of them. Now I was regretting the little white lies I'd told to get here. I'd said I'd worked with animals. Well, I had worked with ani-mals a bit – with my dad's horses when I was a young girl. But that was a long time ago, and horses and pigs aren't the same thing.

'So, what do you have to do?' I asked Mr Coveney, stom-ach knotted, making sure I sounded not bothered.

'You have to go in there and feed them and clean them out.' He was watching me for my reaction. He knew I was upset and frightened.

I was very fit. In the closed prison I'd been running five back-to-back step classes a day. But the pigs looked like they weighed 90 kilos each, and they weren't going to move just because I wanted them to. I wasn't just apprehensive now. I was scared. The thought crossed my mind – what would I have to do to get taken back?

We kept on walking.

And that's when I saw Biddy. We turned round a corner and I saw this beautiful pink and black saddleback sow, just standing on her own in the middle of the yard. I could see she was confused, upset. I looked at her, and she looked back at me. She had these sad big eyes, really expressive. They said: I'm well pissed off. She didn't want to be there. That was how I was feeling too.

'What's up with her?' I said.

'Oh, she's had her babies took off her today.'

I thought about it. She was used to having her babies all around her, and then they were just gone. One minute she was a mum, dozing in the sun with eight little mouths sucking on her; the next minute, standing all on her own in the middle of an empty farmyard.

And something just clicked. There was a connection there. I felt choked up, for her and for me. I kept on looking at her and she kept on looking at me, and I just knew. I thought, I want to do this. I want to come and look after you. If I can't do it, I can't do it, but I'm going to give it my best shot. Love at first sight.

I took a deep breath. Which was a mistake, because it still smelt of shit whether I'd fallen in love with a pig or not. I said to Mr Coveney, 'Yeah, no problem, I'll do it.'

And I went back to my dorm, and I lay on my bed and I couldn't wait to come back in the morning and look after those pigs.

1

DADDY'S LITTLE PRINCESS

My whole life nearly, except when I was in prison, I've lived in Romford in Essex. I was born at five o'clock in the morning, in Rush Green Hospital in Dagenham, on 14 October 1964. I was a small baby – 5 pounds 14 ounces – my mum's still got my little tag. She didn't keep anything else though. No baby book saying what my first word was and that. No newborn baby photos – the first one is of me sitting up – even though there's baby photos of my younger brother Gary. Normally it's the other way around, isn't it? I was the firstborn – where's the pictures of me then? There are only two stories about me as a baby that I can recall. One is, that I was hard to conceive and worse to carry. My mum had pre-eclampsia – she called me a toxic baby – and was in and out of hospital the whole pregnancy. And the other is that I was one of those toddlers that people used to hate having round their houses. Supposedly I was a right little horror; I'd go

round touching all their ornaments, opening all their draw-
ers, climbing on the furniture:'If you're coming, don't bring
her round.' I've always been a problem.

My mum was twenty when she had me, and my dad was
twenty-two. They'd been married for three years and they
were living on a caravan site with no running water.

My mum, Caroline Ann Brooksbank, known as Carol, was
born in York in 1944. She was number ten out of twelve children: Hilda, Rhoda, Louie and Ivy – they both died as
babies – Gladys, Dolly, Malcolm, Derek, David – who was
actually Rhoda's war baby, but my nan brought him up as her
own – my mum Carol, Johnny and Janet. My nan, Louie, was
pregnant eleven times between the ages of twenty and forty-
four. She died in 1963 at the age of sixty, the year before I was
born, when my mum was nineteen years old. My mum's dad,
Harry Brooksbank, came from a large wealthy Tadcaster
family and worked for himself as a coal merchant. He died at
the age of forty-four of lung cancer, when my mum was
three years old. My Auntie Janet, the baby, had been born in
the January and he died in the September.

My mum didn't have a very good childhood. The older
children remembered being quite well off and told stories
about going to church in beautiful matching dresses. But
after my grandad died, my nan had to bring up all the little
ones on her own, in a two-bedroomed house, on widow's
pension and family allowance, plus the money she got from
the American airman who'd knocked up Rhoda. The younger
children grew up with nothing. At Christmas, my mum
remembers going to the courthouse and there would be a

parcel left there, with a present for each child and an apple and an orange.

The oldest brother Malcolm was a drinker and treated all the younger ones, including my mum, really badly.

When Mum was fifteen, in 1959, she came down south to live with one of her older sisters, Gladys, and Gladys's husband, Bob. She got a job as a junior cashier at Wilson's, which was a ladies' fashion store in Romford. After that, she was never very close to her brothers and sisters – who stayed up in York – only with Gladys and Janet and Johnny, the ones who came down south.

As a teenager Mum used to go to a cafe in Collier Row where all the scoundrels and villains hung out on motorbikes. One Sunday when she was sixteen, she was having a cup of tea there with a girlfriend and she got chatting to a bloke called Doug, who would have been eighteen. Doug asked her out for a bet with his mate, and it went from there. That was the April. She married him in the October, at seventeen, had me at twenty, and then my brother Gary came along two years later.

When I was little Mum looked like a young girl, not like a mum. She was very good-looking, and she was a flirt which caused quite a lot of problems. She had long dark hair, lovely long legs, and she used to flaunt herself, wearing hot pants and that, or doing her hair up just to go to the cafe.

She wasn't a kissy, cuddly, huggy kind of mum. We weren't really that kind of family. And looking back it must have been a struggle for her – she was very young, she didn't have her own mum to help, and my dad wasn't around much. If I want to picture her happy back then, I think about her looking after her garden, or breeding her Yorkshire terriers, or flirting with other men.

My dad, Douglas Robert Mackness, was born and bred in Romford like me. He's one of eight – six brothers and two sisters – and they all went to Chase Cross School, which was quite rough. The Macknesses were always a well-known family round here.

My dad's mum was very strict from what I can remember – she died when I was about eight years old. My dad's dad, my grandad, I never really took to. He was a sarcastic bastard, and always having affairs with the women in the betting office where he worked, and he gave my nan a bit of a dog's life. When Dad was about fifteen, my grandad brought a kid home, Dennis, and my nan had to bring this kid up, because it was his kid, and the mum had died. All the other brothers never took to this Dennis; they didn't class him as their brother and they hated him for the fact that their mum had to look after him. I remember Dad crying when my nan died but there were no tears when my grandad died.

How Dad got into the business he was in when I was growing up was by pure chance really. When he was about fifteen, his best friend got given an air rifle for Christmas. And they were playing with it, and it went off, and it blew my dad's left eye out. And because this friend's dad felt responsible – and because Dad's family was known, and feared, in Collier Row – he always looked out for him after that. He let Dad come and work for him on his stall at Romford Market, and then when he died he left the stall to my dad. The friend with the air rifle didn't come out quite so good. He married one of Dad's sisters, had five kids with her. But, back then when no one was doing it, he was into speed. He got drunk and drugged up at a party one night, had a row with Dad's sister, ran off, lay in the gutter all night, and died of hypothermia.

I didn't really know any of my grandparents, but I was always close with my mum's two sisters who came down south, Gladys and Janet.

Auntie Gladys was a bit like a nan to me I suppose. She had a son the same age as Mum, and she was quite like me. When I was in my twenties, the two of us used to go on holiday together to Spain and get up to all sorts of mischief. Like, we'd have our dinner in our hotel, go up to our rooms and get changed, and come downstairs and have another dinner!

Auntie Janet married my dad's brother Malcolm – two sisters married two brothers. But when I was about eighteen, Malcolm started going out snookering every night. Well, I wasn't stupid, no one goes to snooker every night of the week, and when he came back there was no chalk on his cue. I paid for a private detective to follow him to catch him out, and that was the end of that marriage. In hindsight I wish I'd turned a blind eye because I suppose I caused that break-up.

As a child I spent a lot of time at Janet's house. In those days, and even now, I could take my problems to her. Sometimes aunties can be more understanding than mums.

When I was about five months old we moved out of the caravan site to a council flat in Gidea Park and from there quite quickly to a little second-floor flat on Hillrise Road in Collier Row, near Dad's mum. Collier Row is like a working-class suburb of Romford; not very big but you could safely do your weekly shop there. It still today has a Wimpy Bar – of which I have fond memories – and it had a couple of schools, a library, banks, a few restaurants, pubs, and the Collier Row cafe where my mum and dad met. There's a couple of quite well-known high-rise estates too.

My first memories are from that time. One is of shoes. Mum used to take me to her friend's house up the road when I was just a toddler – two or three. They used to trick me. They would take me to the bedroom and get out all the friend's shoes for me to play with. I remember thinking one time, I know Mum's going to do a runner now, because they've got the shoes out. And I ran out into the next room. But she'd already gone. I didn't know then, but those were the days she was visiting my dad in prison.

And the other, I would have been about three years old, is him coming home from prison. I was standing at the top of some concrete steps and he was walking towards me, carrying this big see-through bag with 'HM Prison' on it. They're a collector's item now, those bags. In those days though, you would know if someone had just got out because they'd be at a train station holding a see-through bag. And I knew he was coming home. He hadn't been there, and now he was.

When I was four, and Gary would have been two, Mum got a brand-new three-bedroom house on a new estate in Harold Wood. They had knocked a load of prefabs down and built what must have been three hundred brand-new houses. Harold Wood was a move up in the world. It had bigger houses and a hospital.

It was lovely the day we moved in, we were so excited. I still remember it, everything was new – new carpet, the same pattern all through the house, my mum's first brand-new washing machine, new big colour telly, and a garden, which we hadn't had before. And every family that moved in on the street were all our age, so as we got older there was always a group of kids for us to play with.

We had a little den at the back of the garages. And we used to all play out there, or on the street, just hanging around, playing knock down ginger, swapping stickers, riding our bikes. I had a Chopper and Gary had a Grifter.

My favourite thing on telly was *Little House on the Prairie* – I used to run home from school to watch that. And I liked Rolf Harris, The Monkees, *Wacky Races*, *Why Don't You?*, *Crackerjack* ('... it's Friday, it's five to five ... it's *Crackerjack*'), *Multi-Coloured Swap Shop* on a Saturday, and John Wayne films on a Sunday. I did like *Doctor Who* too, except the Daleks scared me.

One day, when I was six and Gary was four, Mum and Dad took us to a farm in South Ockenham – they were buying something for the market stall, I don't know what. It was Victor Maddern's farm, the actor, only he wasn't there, there was no one there but the four of us. And while Mum and Dad were sorting it out, loading it into their van, whatever it was, we went running around the place, in the early evening light.

We came across a circular brick wall, about the size of a dining table, two, three feet high, with a concrete base. And we were running along the top of the wall, round and round in circles, and climbing in and out, in and out. And my brother said, 'Oh look, this side's come up.' And I jumped on the bit of the base that had come up, and it crumbled under me, and I fell down with the crumbling concrete, ten foot down into the deep, dark, murky water in this well.

I can still remember being in that black water clutching at nothing – and seeing my anorak spreading out on the water, keeping me afloat. And seeing Gary, four-year-old Gary, looking over the top of the wall and trying to decide what to do – watching me for a while, watching me disappear under the water.

My brother ran to where Mum and Dad were. 'You'd better come. Tracy's disappeared, under the water.'

'Where is it, where is it, take me, take me there!' shouted my dad.

And I remember going down under the water and touching the bottom, and clawing at the sides, and coming up and going down again, and my little short life – birthday parties and favourite dogs – flashing past me. I was only six – I didn't know at the time that that meant I was nearly dead.

And they came running over, and Dad jumped straight in. He was feeling in the filthy black water for me, and he grabbed me and slung me up in the air and Mum got hold of me and pulled me out. Mum shouted down to Dad that I was all right, I was still breathing. But it was so deep, Dad couldn't touch the bottom either, and we were the only ones there on that farm. So, with my four-year-old brother in shock and me nearly drowned, Mum had to go and get a hosepipe and tie it onto the van and Dad had to haul himself out.

Then he drove the four or five miles home, and got all his day's takings out of his pockets and hung it on the line to dry.

I was off school for a week after that, quite ill, and the school made me stand up and tell everybody about it in assembly. And a couple of weeks later, we read in the local paper that two brothers had been found dead at the bottom of a well. We all thought: that would have been us two, if Gary had fallen down with me instead of staying up and running for help.

Mum and Dad made sure we both learnt to swim that summer.

From when I was about seven or eight years old, we used to go to Saturday morning pictures. I was the oldest so I would always be in charge. I used to take about six other kids on the 247A bus through Gidea Park and into Romford – my little brother Gary, and some other boys from our road. First we'd go to British Home Stores and buy all our sweets from the pick 'n' mix, and big bags of Wotsits, and a little carton of drink each. I'd have written a list of what we were going to buy. Then we'd walk back to the early morning pictures in South Street. My favourite was the Famous Five. Afterwards, I'd take them across the road for chips. Then we'd get another bus to Romford Market, and congregate around my dad's stall and cause him aggravation. My dad and my mum would be so busy that he'd give me money to take them all away again.

I wanted to help though. I just wanted to be where he was, doing what he was doing. 'Can I help, Dad? Can I do it? Please can I?' And from about eight or nine, he let me. In those days, back in its heyday, Romford Market was manic, heaving – it was the place to be. It was one of the busiest markets there ever was – Wednesdays, Fridays and Saturdays. People came there from miles around. There were probably three or four hundred stalls all around the square, mostly families selling fruit and veg, meat, fish, nuts, sweets, biscuits, clothes, shoes, toiletries, dog food, all trying to outdo each other, shouting the loudest, getting the customers' attention. Even at six o'clock in the morning it was buzzing, with the vans all trying to unload before a certain time, their reverse lights beeping, drivers arguing with each other about who had to get out of whose way. Most weeks there would be a physical fight, and there was always a drama – someone's husband would come back to his stall drunk and the wife would be screaming at him, or some stallholder was having an affair with some other stallholder's daughter.

Next door to my dad's stall was Fancotts, a wet fish stall, with live eels out the back in a tank, and the whole square smelt of the frying onions from the hot dog stands.

I shouted what my dad shouted: 'Come on, Mum, get your plums. Come on, Mum, get your bananas in their pyjamas.' It was crazy, exciting, and I felt like I belonged.

I always wanted to be with him, but he wasn't around much for one reason or another through these years. He was a really bad gambler and he was into all kinds of illegal activities to help fund it – silly things, handling stolen goods, things like that. He was in and out of prison all the time I was growing up. As a young girl, I just took it for granted that everyone went to visit men in prison.

And then even when he was around, he wasn't around if you know what I mean. His routine was, he used to go out at three o'clock in the morning and go to the fruit and veg market in London or Stratford to buy all the veg for his stall and shops. At first he just had the stall on Romford Market, but later he got a chance to buy a couple of shops, one on the Collier Row roundabout and a farm shop further down the road, and he got people in to manage them. All he wanted to do was go and get the fruit and veg. He'd be done by maybe eight o'clock, go for his breakfast in the Collier Row cafe, and then he'd go and spend all day with his horses on his farm outside Ockenham. In the afternoon he might go down the betting office or the casino. And he'd come home about seven or eight o'clock at night and fall asleep in his chair.

What little time he was around, he would spend most of it arguing with my mum. Sometimes it felt like that was all they ever did. Me and Gary hated it.

They would argue because he was never there.

They would argue over money. Mum was very money-oriented, maybe because growing up she never had anything. Every Sunday afternoon when Dad and his brother Dennis would count up the week's takings, Mum would see the money and start on about her share.

They argued about Mum's Valium tablets. She was on them for years and Dad hated it. One time, when I was about nine, he flushed them down the toilet.

'What did you fucking do that for?'

'Because you're out of it all the time.'

'I need them, the life you're leading me. You're never here.'

Screaming, shouting, crying. I was sitting at the top of the stairs.

'Tracy!' my mum shouted. I came down. 'Go to Tommy's mum down the road and ask her can I have some of her Valium please.'

The worst though was when she flirted and Dad got jealous. She used to instigate things on purpose. We hardly ever went out anywhere, they were always too tired. But any time we did, to a family funeral maybe, or a horse show, or Guy Fawkes' night at my nan's, I would be on edge, living on my nerves. It put a black cloud over everything. She'd start attracting too much attention, or talking to someone for too long, or dancing with someone, and there would be a big scene. He'd come over and grab her. Or slap her. I used to hope we could stay for the whole party but we always left early.

There was a lot of money around. We were quite spoilt in that way. Well known in the street for it.

Like, we always had all matching clothes and that. Immaculately turned out, people used to comment on it. Sometimes Mum'd have stuff made up for me because I was quite big. Once she bought a coat from Debenhams for £100 – that's probably about £1000 now – never even wore it.

And she always had nice stuff for the house, always the best. A really expensive three-piece suite from the best shop in Romford, and a big top-of-the-range wall cabinet with glass in it for all her old shit, you know, like tea sets and china dolls and horses and that.

My dad always had a nice car – a Rover that smelt of the leather seats, with a big cassette player, or a Jag. The thing I most remember from his car though is being whacked in it. Me and Gary were fighting in the back. My dad had switched off from it, he was listening to his Roy Orbison, but my mum was screeching, 'Are you going to do something about them?' Over and over. Until he stopped the car, got out, opened the back door, and smacked both of us. Then it was 'Don't hit them, don't hit them.'

At Christmas we'd have so many presents, and me and Gary would add up what they came to. If I thought he had a lot more than me there'd be murders. He'd always get a motorbike – a little scrambler, a Yamaha 50 or something, five hundred quid – and I'd get jewellery, a sovereign on a chain and things like that. Everyone else on the street got a push-bike, he got a motorbike.

For my birthdays, for about four or five years, Mum would take us to Bumbles restaurant on South Street in Romford. It was like a Wimpy, like an American diner; this was before McDonald's hit the scene. I would be allowed to take a few friends with me, and we'd have burgers, and then they would bring out a cake and sing 'Happy Birthday'.

And every Monday Dad would buy us £5 worth of sweets. That was a lot of sweets. And we'd put them in the cupboard and that would last us all week. Pink Panther chocolate bars, and them necklaces on an elastic that you'd put round your neck and eat the little hard sweets off, and sherbet Dip Dabs – a liquorice stick that you dipped into a load of sher-bet – and Space Dust that fizzled on your tongue and Black Jacks and Fruit Salads and Cough Candys and Bon Bons.

We were the first family in the school to go on holiday to
Spain. We used to go to Magaluf in Mallorca, and stay in a
five star hotel called the Coral Playa every year for ten years,
from when I was six years old. We'd always go in June, when
we should have been at school taking our end-of-year
exams, and there would be the same children there every
year, from all different countries, and because we were regular clients they would come up and shake our hands and
make a big fuss of us. The hotel had a lift down the cliff face
to the beach, and every night there would be music on and
we'd all get up – the girls in long dresses and the boys in
white shirts – and dance. And there would be a beauty contest each week. So in the first week, my mum would win it,
and she'd be 'Miss Coral Playa'. We'd go to bed and in the
morning there would be the big bouquet of flowers and the
bloody sash. And then in the second week, she'd be invited
to be a judge. About four years in a row.

I enjoyed infants school, but I wasn't happy in the juniors. I
was quite a chubby child and I used to get called names. I
wasn't bullied exactly, nothing as much as that, but I felt
uncomfortable with myself. I wasn't happy with what I was.
I was confident and bossy at home, but I was shy at school,
and I didn't have friends there, didn't move in a big gang.
When I was ten or eleven, there were a couple of girls on our
street who were always teasing me about being tubby and
we would fight a lot – but not proper fighting, just how girls
do. Then one day, I lost it with one of these girls and I beat
her right up. After that things were different. All the kids saw
what I was capable of doing and they left me alone. And I felt

different about myself too. I know what I was capable of. I knew I could handle myself. And I learnt, even at that early age, a lesson about reputation and giving off a persona that will keep people away from you, stop them messing with you.

After I was about ten, we used to go on our holidays to Spain without Dad, because he had to stay behind to look after his horses. One year, when I was about twelve, he turned up unexpectedly. He'd rung Mum up in Spain and said he needed his passport. He was on bail for something or other and said his solicitor wanted his passport, and where was it? And the next day Mum was sitting on the beach in her bikini, chatting to some geezer who me and Gary had been calling Mr Fancy Pants – who was there on his own with his kid. I'd gone back to the hotel room for something, and our room was on the same floor as the reception, and I was walking back along the corridor and out of the big glass window I saw a coach pull up and I saw Dad get off the coach. I was petrified. I ran down to the beach and screamed, 'Mum, quick, quick, Dad's here!' and she managed to move away from Mr Fancy Pants before Dad got there.

And it would have been OK, but we were only young, me and Gary, and we kept saying, 'Oh look, there's Mr Fancy Pants,' and one night Dad just flipped. They had a big fight in our hotel room, and Dad got Mum by the throat and I thought he was going to throw her over the balcony. Then he got out his knife, went downstairs, and got Mr Fancy Pants by the throat too.

He was very insecure, and probably, looking back, he was right to be.

My dad got his shop on the Collier Row roundabout when I was eleven, and the farm shop soon afterwards. He didn't want to do the Romford Market stall himself anymore, so he let it out to a couple called Bert and Joan. Mum and my dad's brother Trevor managed the Collier Row shop, with me helping on Saturdays for £15 a day, and Dad's brother Dennis managed the farm shop for him.

That freed Dad up for the horses.

Over the summer, we used to spend the weekends going to horse shows, and staying in the little accommodation he'd rigged up inside the horsebox.

Poor Gary hated it – he was always terrified of horses after he fell out of a horse and trap into a ditch. You can tell on all the photos he didn't want to be there. And it used to cause arguments with Mum again. 'You're jealous of the horses,' Dad would say.

'I'm not jealous of the horses. But the home should come first. You pay a thousand, two thousand pounds on a horse and trap, people think you're rich, but we're still living in a council house.'

But I loved the horse shows; they were what I looked forward to.

The shows would run all over the country, every weekend, from May to September. The first one was the Easter Parade in Regent's Park in London, with hundreds of people with horses and carts – they're not allowed to do that in Regent's Park anymore – and then the Watford Show, the South of

England Show, the Harlow Show sponsored by Gilbey's gin, and one on Clapham Common.

We started preparing on the Wednesday, when Dad would get someone down to plait the hackney horses' manes and tails, and put the pompoms on. On the Thursday night, he would get out the three sets of harnesses in the kitchen, and he and his man George would spend all evening cleaning and polishing them. Friday night he'd brush the horses and bath them – get the hosepipe all over them and Fairy Liquid, or proper horse shampoo, and hope they didn't go and roll in a load of old shit straight afterwards. Five o'clock on the Saturday morning it was like a military operation – load the horsebox, load the horses, pack all the horse feed and everything else we needed for the two days.

You would always see the same people at the shows. It would be the same competitors, different judges. When we arrived, I'd always want to check first whether the boy I had a crush on was there. And then I loved wandering round and looking at the stalls, and eating in the showman's tent, and staying up late with all the other kids, seeing what we could nick, hanging around the show ground and sitting together at the showman's bar at night.

Sometimes Mum wouldn't come and I used to be the little housewife, trying to cook us breakfast and dinner on the two-ring gas stove in the musty horsebox where we ate and slept. I remember going and buying the sausages, thinking, These must be the best sausages, because they're in the showman's tent. One time I even managed to cook us a roast dinner. It took me about nine hours, but I did it.

When I was about thirteen, Dad decided I was going to compete in the shows. He bought me a little grey horse, Charlie, and two different traps – a two-wheel private driving trap, and a costermonger's cart (a red and yellow painted fruit and veg barrow) that we could enter in the trade class – and two different sets of harnesses. My dad sent me away to stay with a woman called Georgina Brush in a little old-fashioned cottage with a creaky latch in Great Leighs, near Broomfield in Chelmsford. She was one of the top hackney horse lady drivers in the country, right respected on the circuit, very pretty, with long dark hair. I lived with her for three or four weeks, her and her young son. It was quite an adventure.

She taught me how to drive hackney horses properly – horses that step up high; they seem to float if you do it right. At first, all I could do was hold the reins in my fists. That was fine for trade class, but Georgina Brush taught me to drive properly, elegantly, with the reins threaded through my fingers, and just a little tiny movement to make the horse turn or reverse.

Now I would go with my dad over to his farm in South Ockenham most days after school and at the weekends, to exercise Charlie, and groom him. And now when we got to the shows I had my own jobs to do. I had to clean my little trap, and polish the brass on it with Brasso and Duraglit. I had to clean my harness. Clean the velvet cushions for the trap. I had to put the harness on Charlie, and oil his hooves and wash his tail and make sure he was gleaming.

That year at Harlow it was brilliant weather and there were thousands of people there. We were due in the ring at two o'clock. I spent the morning cleaning and polishing. All the people at the show wandering round could watch me getting him ready. At twelve o'clock I put the harness on Charlie, and his big long collar. At one o'clock I put on my brown trouser suit and my white blouse and my bowler hat with a green feather sticking out of it, and my brown leather driving gloves. Charlie had a thick, thick neck and a little cropped tail because it had got caught in a door when he was younger. He was beautiful. And he used to step really high.

They announced over the tannoy that our class had started, the under-fifteens, and we all stepped into the ring. There were maybe twenty of us that day, all driving our traps around the ring, with the judges in the middle. I was sat bolt upright with the reins threaded through my gloves. I only needed to make tiny movements, Charlie knew what to do. I could hear people saying, 'Here he comes, here comes Charlie,' and I could tell he felt like the cock of the walk. Everyone loved him, and the more they clapped, the more he played up to them, lifting his hooves higher and higher, floating round the ring. The judges called us in and lined us up. When it was our turn to go round the ring on our own, my mouth was dry, my heart was beating out of my chest, and I was hot and bothered in my brown suit. There must have been a thousand people watching us, maybe more. But I drove him round the ring, stopped right in front of the judges, reversed up to show them he would do as he was told.

The announcement came over the tannoy – 'Tracy Mackness and Charlie, first prize.' Everyone was clapping me. I was in the papers. I was full of it.

We got a first at Clapham Common too that year, another really big one. Me and Charlie kept winning and winning. I became the second youngest junior whip in the country. My little Charlie did me proud.

Overall, if someone was to ask me, did I have a happy childhood? I'd say yeah, a lot of it was happy. Up until about the age of thirteen. And then it wasn't really a childhood anymore.

2

'WHAT ARE YOU GOING TO DO ABOUT IT?'

One night when I was thirteen, my dad didn't come home. At two o'clock in the morning I read the order list to Uncle Trevor over the phone so he could go to the market and get the fruit and veg. The next morning, Mum got a call from Dad's solicitor to say he was at the police station. He'd got done again, for cattle rustling this time. Cattle rustling? Me and Mum thought it was a joke. We went down there with some food and fags but they wouldn't let us see him until he'd been charged.

After three days, my dad came home feeling very sorry for himself and told us the whole story. He had nicked a load of pigs and cows and horses from a farm in Wales. Not just that, he'd nicked a cattle box from another farm down there, to drive them all away. Nicked a cattle box from one farm, driven it to another one, loaded up someone else's animals in it, and drove back to Romford. But he'd got greedy. He hadn't sold them on straight away; he'd kept them in his barns on his farm in Ockenham, fattening them up so he'd get a better price for them.

The day he got arrested, he'd had a vet down to the farm to look at one of his horses. There'd been no one else there, and this vet had gone mooching around, opening up a few barns. In one barn he'd found so many pigs they were literally on top of one another. In another there were a load of cattle. By the time my dad got to the farm at four o'clock in the afternoon, the police had it surrounded. They found a lorry-load of Swarfega there too – the really expensive hand-wash mechanics and that use – and confiscated that.

His trial was about seven or eight months later, in Chelmsford. I hated going to it. He went not guilty.

They found him guilty, and it was on the whole front page of the *Romford Recorder*.

That's when I stopped going to school. I was embarrassed, because I was the only girl at school with a dad in prison. And for such a ridiculous thing too. This was Romford, not the Wild West.

Everyone at school knew. Not that I care now, but I did care then. I knew they were talking behind my back even though they were told in assembly not to say anything. I was walking to school one day and I heard two boys behind me laughing about it.

And, anyway, I couldn't go to school because I had to help pick up the pieces for running my dad's businesses – the stall, the shops and the horses. As far as I was concerned, I just had to get on with it. No choice in the matter.

Between us – me, my mum, and my dad's brothers Trevor and Dennis – we'd have to do it all as best we could. Trevor took over the buying, and I helped out wherever I was needed – at the Collier Row shop with Mum, or the farm shop with Dennis, or with the horses. I couldn't drive yet, so someone would pick me up and take me to where I needed to be. We had to get rid of the Swarfega too. He got not guilty on that and one day the police delivered it all back to Mum's house on our little turning, a lorry-load of big forty-gallon drums.

The worst was the stallion horses. They were really strong and vicious. I'd seen one of them sink their teeth into Dad's leg one time and toss him around and turn him upside down, and we'd had to use pitchforks to get him off. My dad was fourteen, fifteen stone. And I used to have to go in there, petrified, and feed them. I had no choice, there was no one else.

So I didn't have time for school, or for chatting about fashion and clothes, or for the youth club that everyone else at school had suddenly started talking about all the time.

The horse shows all stopped too, because we had no means of getting there.

And that was the end of my childhood really. Most young teenage girls around that age, they go upstairs one day a nice child and come down a monster who you don't know anymore. Well I actually felt the change happening in me – like I'd been taken over by aliens or something. Except, with me, I went upstairs a child and came down a grown-up. Because I had to. My dad was in prison, and I realised I had to take responsibility.

*

I was so headstrong, there wasn't really much anyone could do about me and school, even if they'd wanted to. Mum couldn't control me, hadn't been able to for years. Even when she did hit me, it never hurt. She'd finish and I'd say, 'You'd better try harder than that.' She couldn't do anything with me.

Dad tried to hit me when I visited him in prison one day. 'You'd better go to school,' he said. But he was on one side of the table and I was on the other, so what was he going to do?

'Don't get all flash and that with me,' I said. 'I'm not going. What are you going to do about it?' I used to goad him, because I knew he wasn't allowed to touch me in there.

Finally the School Board went mad. They'd cut me some slack at the beginning because of my dad being in prison and us struggling without him. Then they'd started coming round the house every other day. We would pretend not to be in but sometimes they'd catch us out. After I hadn't been to school for a whole year, they took Mum to court. They couldn't take Dad to court because he was in prison. No big deal, it's only court. She got fined £50 and I had to pay it out of my earnings but I didn't care. I thought that was that problem out of the way.

But when I still didn't go to school, the School Board took me to court – not Mum, but me, aged fourteen. I stood up in front of the magistrate and she told me she understood it was hard for me, but if I didn't go to school she would put a care order on me. The options were laid out. Either I went back to school, or, if I didn't go, they'd have no choice but to put me into care. 'And then', she warned, 'you will go to school.'

I had to take it seriously then. I was going to have to go back for a bit. But I wasn't going to comply with anything I didn't have to.

The first day, to make sure I went, they sent this dear little old School Board man to take me in his car. It was embarrassing.

I'd been away for a year and I'd grown up in that time, I wasn't the same girl that had left at thirteen. I felt like I was different from how I'd been, and different from all the others – I was above all of that now. I looked different too. I'd had my hair permed, I'd lost weight, and I was wearing my version of the uniform, not theirs. If I was going back, it was going to be on my terms, head held high. I wore the grey skirt, but skintight and with a big split up to here, the way I wanted it. And just a short-sleeved blouse and a little short tie. No socks. And green moccasins with a leather sole and a little lace on them, when it was supposed to be black shoes. When I walked in, the boys were like 'Woaaahhhh' – they couldn't believe it was me.

They made me sit some exams my first day back. I'd always got out of exams before, because me and my brother Gary, we were very manipulative, and we always used to persuade Mum to take us on our holidays to Spain at the end of term so we wouldn't have to sit them. So I'd always been in the bottom set because I'd never taken any exams. But they caught me out this time and made me sit them. I got such high marks they put me up to the O-level group. Back then, there were two different exams where now everyone takes GCSEs – there was CSEs for the less bright kids, and O-levels for the clever ones. My marks had even been higher than lots of the kids in the O-level group, who'd been to school and studied for the exams.

Well, that made things even worse. At least in the CSE group everyone else just wanted to mess about like I did. And I'd had my friends in that group, rebels like me. We used to go out of school at lunchtime, even though you weren't allowed to, and go round my friend's house and get up to mischief. Like rummaging through her mum and dad's bedroom and looking at their dirty mags and that. It broke the day up, made it not so bad going back in the afternoon.

But the O-level group was the sensible group – they wanted to work, and learn – it was a different thing. It bored me shitless, and they weren't my type of person. They didn't understand the problems we had at home, and they would talk about silly things on the telly, or the youth club, and I didn't have a clue what they were on about half the time.

What I hated most of all was when a teacher would dig me out and try to make me answer a question. Because at school I was quite shy, believe it or not. Headstrong, but shy. So even though I knew the answer, I wouldn't answer it. I used to get really embarrassed and go bright red. And once any teacher had done that to me, that was it. I couldn't stand them from then on, wouldn't have anything to do with them.

I just didn't want to be there. It wasn't that I couldn't do it. I was very bright. And I wasn't naughty either. It was just, I knew what I wanted to do, and this wasn't it.

*

I stuck it for a few weeks. Got the School Board man off my back. I think he was petrified of me and delighted to sign off on my case. Then, from the age of about fourteen and a half, I just stopped going. I would go into school in the morning and get my mark in the register. And then I'd be on the bus at ten past nine, on the way to my dad's shop in Collier Row and then to the farm to get the horses fed.

They used to all watch me out of their classrooms, walking across the playground, out the gates. And, obviously, my mark was never there in the afternoon. They must have known exactly what I was doing. But I think by that time, everyone, all the teachers, had just given up on me. Not one of them ever stopped me in the playground and asked me where I was going; they were probably putting the afternoon mark in themselves, just to stop the aggravation. I don't blame them – they probably thought it's better for everyone. Because I'd made it quite clear I was going to wear my uniform not theirs, and I'd made it quite clear I couldn't stand most of the teachers and I didn't want to be there, and I must have been their worst nightmare.

My dad came out of prison, but he didn't make me go back.

I would go back occasionally, on my own terms.

I loved netball, absolutely loved it, loved it, lived for it. I was a brilliant shooter; I could get the ball in from anywhere in the circle, the furthest point, and everywhere we went, playing other schools, we used to thrash them all. The school even gave me a netball post to put in my garden so I could practise at home. So I used to not go to school for a month but then I'd go back for a netball match – get on the minibus with the others at lunchtime and go and play. The netball tutor was one of the few teachers I did like.

I was happy with my life. Fruit and veg and horses. And boys.

I loved working in my dad's shops. I was earning good money – thirty or forty quid a day – and I threw myself into it, took it more seriously than he did. I didn't mind getting out of bed early in the morning to unload lorry-loads of potatoes, or another time to shift 3000 Christmas trees.

One time when I could have been only fourteen, I was in the Collier Row cafe with my dad. We were sitting eating our breakfasts and it was time to go and open up his farm shop down the road. I wanted to go. I was nagging him, 'Come on, we've gotta go, we've gotta go and open the shop up.' And he was trying to put me off. 'In a minute, in a minute.' So I just got up, got in his orange van and drove it up the road. All in second gear, and quite a lot of grinding, but I got myself there. The men in the cafe were killing themselves – 'You do know your daughter's just drove off' – and he had to get one of them to give him a lift up there.

I taught myself to drive after that, felt like I needed to be able to do it.

That caused a few little incidents. I taught myself on my dad's Mercedes A-series van and my mum's Mini, and I smashed them both up.

I managed to knock the door off the van as I was driving it round and round the farm shop one time. It was one of those side doors that go out and along and I'd been speeding around the farm with it open and hit a tractor. I was so scared to tell my dad, I threw the door into the back of the van and parked it up against the wall.

I was going to tell him that afternoon at the horse show, but I bottled it. I was shitting it all afternoon, all night. Dad went out at three o'clock in the morning as usual to do the buying, took the fruit and veg to the farm shop, and found the van. He knew straight away it was me. Seven o'clock in the morning I was in bed and he came storming in, shouting and screaming, 'I'm gonna kill you, I'm gonna kill you, look what you done.'

My mum was going, 'What, what, what?'

I said, 'It wasn't me. Someone drove in and knocked the door off and drove out again.'

No way he believed me. 'That's it,' he said, 'you're paying for it.' But I wouldn't. And because he wouldn't either, he ended up welding it back on himself. It never opened after that and to get in the back you had to go in the other side.

It caused a few problems with Dad's brother Dennis, me being so involved with the business when I was so young. Dennis had worked for my dad for a long time, running his shops, and he hated the fact that there was a young girl there bossing him about. He used to storm off on a regular basis. One particular Saturday, in the farm shop, we had a big row because he'd tried to sell cheaper to one of his friends and I'd walked up to him and said, 'It doesn't come to that, it comes to this.' I'd undermined him in front of everyone, and he just got in his car and drove off. Dad wasn't there, he'd done his bit for the day buying the fruit and veg and gone off to his horses or wherever, and mobile phones hadn't been invented then. So I had no choice – I just had to stay there and run the shop on my own all day. When Dad came back, he couldn't believe it, but I'd had no way of telling him what was going on.

About this time, a boy called Johnnie Fenton started coming into the farm shop every now and again. He was friends with one of the boys who worked there on a Saturday and he used to screech up to the shop in his fast little Mini van. I couldn't not notice him. He was about eighteen, tall and really skinny, with curly brown hair and an earring and he always wore skin-tight jeans and dealer boots. He had a motorbike and was ready for a fight; everyone knew him, he was a boy about town.

Johnnie was really helpful. He'd do anything you asked him. He started taking Gary to motocross, and then he started offering to give me lifts over to my dad's farm which is when it started between him and me.

We began to rely on him quite a lot and he ended up staying over at our house now and again. Mum quite liked him because he didn't take any nonsense from me. He used to slap me round the head if I backchatted Mum – 'Don't talk to your mother like that' – to keep me in check.

I knew it was coming, the pressure had been building up for a while; it was always there. One day at our house, we were in my bedroom and one thing led to another. It just sort of happened. Nothing was said. I remember thinking God, what is all the fuss about? We were together for about a year after that.

Dad didn't much like Johnnie. He said, 'You've got a

choice, you can have boys or horses.' And I said, 'I'll have boys.' But I had them both.

When Dad got out of prison, we started the horse shows again. I wanted to go up into the proper hackney class and he bought me a little hackney pony. She was a bit skittish though – she had a mind of her own. I would take her into the ring and she would just prance around. You couldn't be judged on that.

And I didn't need to be at school, because as far as I was concerned this was what I was going to do my whole life. I was going to have my own shop – my dad's shop – and work for myself. I was set up. That's what I thought.

But then when I was fifteen, Dad got nicked again. I think this time it was for handling stolen goods. That changed a lot of things.

First the horses went. He sold them this time when he knew he was going to prison. So that was the end of that. No more Charlie, no more prizes, no more good times with my little friends.

Then Mum found some new mates – somewhere, I don't know where – neighbours in the street or something. And even though she wasn't single really, she started going out and about with her new friends to these singles clubs and over-27s clubs. She got a whole new wardrobe of clothes, and had somewhere different to be every night of the week. I suppose she was still quite young, she would only have been thirty-five, and she hadn't ever gone out and done those things.

Then, inevitably, Mum met a bloke somewhere, and

decided she wanted to be with him. She served divorce papers on Dad while he was in prison. A bit underhand I thought that was, but she'd decided she could do better, and she knew if she did it to his face he'd talk her out of it. That had happened before. When I was about seven, she'd started to divorce him and it had all been going through and then he'd said he'd buy her a new car and she'd changed her mind. I think it was a Mini.

At first, when Dad got out of prison, he came back to live with us, and slept in the same bed with Mum, even though she was divorcing him. The atmosphere in the house was horrendous. He was really angry and jealous and would let down Mum's tyres when she wanted to go out, and then he'd sit up brooding, waiting for her to come back in. Me and my brother Gary just dreaded it. Then the abuse would start, the rowing and shouting. And they'd fight, physically fight.

One time I woke up in the middle of the night and heard screaming. I looked out of my bedroom window and saw the two of them, my mum and dad, fighting in the street, with her screaming. I was so frightened for Mum, I ran out of the house naked, two o'clock in the morning, to try to stop it. Sixteen years old and my dad saw me naked.

And then, after this had been going on for about two or three months, one day he just left and moved into a mobile home in Collier Row.

At first we thought he'd just found somewhere else to live and we were relieved.

A week later, I passed my driving test. It was a big deal

because now I didn't have to rely on other people to get me here, there and everywhere. He was supposed to come round and see me – he'd promised to buy me a little car if I passed. But he didn't come. I started ringing round all his friends and I got nowhere with them; they were all a bit evasive. I rang the bloke who lived opposite him but I got no joy from him either. So I decided to get a taxi up to the mobile home site and wait for him in his caravan. I waited and waited and waited. It was getting dark by the time I heard his van pull up, and I ran out.

He had a bird sitting next to him in the van.

When I saw her there, I went mad. I started screaming at both of them. I grabbed her door, but she'd locked it. I wanted to pull her out of the van and hit her. I was scream-ing and pulling at the door, banging on the window. She was sat on the other side, watching me, looking petrified. Dad came out and tried to get me under control but I wouldn't be calmed down.

I walked off and Dad came after me in the van. After a big scuffle he got me in and took me home. He told me he'd met this girl down the betting office or the casino or something. Her name was Jean.

When Mum found out, she drove down there one night, throwing all his clothes and boots out the car window as she went down the Lower Bedfords Road. She realised then that she'd made a mistake splitting up with him, but it was too late. Within two months Jean was pregnant and they'd bought a place near Stansted Airport.

Dad sold all his businesses and disappeared out of our lives. We were left with nothing. Complete limbo. I felt completely let down. Everything I'd thought I was going to do in my life, I couldn't do.

I was sixteen, and I had no qualifications whatsoever, no family business to run, no money coming in, no horses, no dad, nothing. I'd thought everything was all mapped out, and suddenly it wasn't. I didn't know what I was going to do.

3

STELLA

One night, when I was sixteen, and Dad was still in prison, before he left us, I persuaded Mum to take me out clubbing with her. She'd been going out on these singles nights for a few months, and coming home and telling me all about them. And I thought I was quite grown up – I wasn't going to school, I was working my dad's businesses – and I wanted to go out too. In my eyes I knew it all already.

I must have driven her mad asking and asking to come out with her, until one night she let me come. Out with her and her little mates to the British Legion Club on the Western Road in Romford, on a Monday night.

I started getting ready in the afternoon. Pulled all the stops out, got all dolled up in my best gear.

I always liked to have nice clothes, good quality. If you'd opened my wardrobe up back then, everything in there would be Jane Norman. Even though I was young, I was earning good money working for my dad so I never had to go where all the other girls were going, like C&A or whatever. To be honest, I don't know what the cheap shops even were because I would never have dreamed of going into them. For me it was Jane Norman, or Topshop, or Miss Selfridge. Or there was a shop up in Gants Hill called Deborah's, with all over-the-top expensive stuff, and another shop, called Sue's, up in Rainham on the Cherry Tree roundabout, with all one-offs, quite different things, like gold lamé tops, where the Page 3 Girls and footballers' wives all used to go. And I used to have my shoes hand-made at an Italian shop in Upton Park – white and gold, or white and red, the flashier the better – a pair to match each outfit, and no one else had them. I had to have the best quality. I had an absolute horror of walking in somewhere and having the same thing on as someone else. I wanted to be a cut above everyone else, not on the same level. I wanted to stand out.

It was the summer of 1981. My hair was permed and highlighted. I was really brown because I was doing three or four sunbeds a week even though sunbeds were quite new back then, plus I used to buy enhancing cream to make me even browner. I picked out a little tight shiny black miniskirt, and a skin-tight top made out of that stretchy material – not Lycra, this was before Lycra, but the material they still some-times make boob tubes out of, like a load of wiggly elastics covered in glittery gold and black fabric. Stiletto shoes to match the top, my gold and white ones. Bomber jacket. And all my gold jewellery. Not a lot of make-up – I was never much of a make-up person. They did my make-up for me once in Miss Selfridge and I didn't recognise myself. A ton of hairspray though, that's how I liked it, and some of my mum's Opium perfume.

Mum was nagging me to get ready quicker. 'Come on, Tracy, or we won't get in.' The drinks were really cheap on singles night – about a pound a drink – and there was a big crowd of younger blokes who liked to get there early and flash their cash about, so word had spread and now everyone wanted to be there. 'We've got to be there by quarter to eight or we won't get in.'

Seven-thirty, me and mum got into her little white Mini and she drove us down there. She was all dolled up too, immaculate. I was fit, nice figure, and I was looking good with my spiral perm and my matching outfit from Jane Norman – I reckoned I could have been eighteen. I was trying to look older and my mum was trying to look younger. We were both probably hoping we looked like sisters. The two old gimmers on the door barely looked at me though – they took my £2 and gave me a little raffle ticket for my jacket and I was in.

Inside, it was all flock wallpaper and wooden tables, and benches against the wall, really old-fashioned. There was a wooden dance floor, and a DJ, trying to get all the women dancing. It was packed, heaving.

I stuck with my mum at first. I was a bit overawed by the atmosphere and all the blokes there, and everyone getting so tanked up and out on the hunt. Everyone was out looking for someone. Lots of older women looking for free drinks. 'Unmarried mothers,' said Mum. 'And if they get a shag at the end that's a bonus!' Lots of men I knew to be married. And lots of younger blokes too. 'They like the older women because they're so grateful, they don't have to try so hard to pull them. They call it grab-a-granny night.' Just a cattle market really.

Mum pointed out the Adams boys. Five brothers – Darren, Robbie, Ricky, Barry and Mark – all standing together. They were the ones flashing the cash. I knew of them. They were a well-known family in Collier Row, quite big faces. They all had their own little businesses, always wore nice shoes, drove Mercs. There was a crowd of women throwing themselves at them.

Gloria Gaynor came on – 'I Will Survive' – and Mum wanted to dance. I wandered back towards the door, out of the crush. I wasn't that impressed so far. But there was a big row going on – some girls were being turned away, and they were devastated – so I came back and stood at the bar on my own and ordered another vodka and lemonade.

And that's when I saw her. I'll never forget that moment.

It wasn't just me either. It seemed like everyone stopped what they were doing and looked up. Because striding through the door and over to the bar was someone who looked like nothing I'd ever seen before. Everything was bigger, better, flashier. Everything was larger than life.

She was on her own. But it was obvious everyone knew her. She kept walking, and I kept watching. I couldn't take my eyes off her.

She must have been in her mid-thirties and biggish built, with huge peroxide blonde hair piled up on her head, a really made-up face with big red lipstick, the tightest skirt, the highest heels, fishnet stockings and a clingy gold top with frills all over and her tits hanging out the front. False nails, false eyelashes, false everything.

Someone bought her a drink when she got to the bar. Everyone was looking at her – you couldn't fail to look round when she went past, with her heels and her hair she was probably six foot three – and a crowd of men started to form around her. She made some joke I couldn't hear and every-one laughed. I downed my drink and kept watching.

She was brassy and loud and over the top. She stood up on a bar stool and downed a pint of bitter. Half of them cheered, the other half were looking up her skirt and she knew it. She was the centre of attention, attracting more and more people into her circle, holding court, and I was mes-merised.

The group around her at the bar got bigger and bigger; the Adams brothers and their lot joined in, and then someone in my mum's crowd knew someone in her crowd, and our crowds kind of mixed together. The rounds were flowing, me on the vodka, and the centre of attention – Stella – on the Canadian Club whiskey, and before I knew it I was chatting to her.

I wanted to know all about her. She worked for some local millionaire businessman, Jim Whybrew, buying and selling bankrupt stock, she told me in this nasal East End voice – Barbara Windsor but an octave lower. Like, she'd go to Holland and buy old tins of peas or baked beans, stuff like that, 1p a tin, bring them back to England, re-tin them, put a new label on them, sell them on. And this Jim Whybrew bought her a lot of jewellery, and she used to go out and stay with him at his place in Portugal. It was obviously all working out quite well for her, the way she was flashing her money about. And she had a son called Petey who was just a baby, and a teenage daughter and a grown-up son from her first marriage that had ended when she caught him with a barmaid in the local pub. She'd dismantled the bed, taken it to the pub, and thrown it at the two of them. She was out of the East End and she was well known down there.

I listened to her telling me about herself, until chucking-out time, about ten-thirty, quarter to eleven. It was obvious that Stella's night wasn't finished; she was a woman about town, she didn't go home, she went on from there to somewhere else. I wanted a bit of that – I wanted to go on with Stella. So I asked Mum, 'Can I go with Stella to Ilford Palais?'

'I don't think so,' she said. She'd had enough, she was going home, and that meant I had to as well. But I really wanted to stay out.

'Well, you can go home, but can I just go?' I begged. 'Please let me go, please let me go.'

She said, 'No, you're not going, no.' And then she said, 'How are you going to get home?' Brilliant, I thought. That's a maybe.

'I'll get her home,' said Stella.

I jumped into the front seat of Stella's little Mini before my mum could think about it. Eight miles down the road to the Ilford Palais. It was an over-27s night there – three pound to get in, then cheap drinks all night. I might look eighteen, but I didn't look twenty-seven.

But everyone knew her there, all the bouncers and everyone – she was a big face. I was with Stella, and no one was going to stop Stella. We walked straight past the queue, big smiles at the bouncers ('All right, Stel?'), in the door no questions asked, and over to the doubles bar. With all the heads turning, Stella in front being treated like a celebrity and me strutting in behind her, that was it for me. I thought, This is what I want, this is what I'm destined to do.

Inside, there was a massive dance floor, loads of men, another total cattle market. At the doubles bar, there was loads of coppers, and loads of firemen, and Stella knew them all. I don't think we paid for a single drink ourselves, and now I was necking the vodka like there was no tomorrow. I started to attract a lot of attention, especially when I got dancing. By the end of the night I was like the Yellow Pages I had so many phone numbers.

When the Palais closed, at three o'clock in the morning, we went across the road with some of these coppers and firemen to a Greek restaurant and they gave me hummus and vine leaves and taramasalata. Another new thing I'd never experienced before. With all the vodka and the rich food, when I got home I was sick in my mum's front room. I was spewing up and I wanted to die and it was all over the carpet and my mum had to clear it up.

But when I woke up the next day, my first thought was, When am I going out again?

It was the start of one of the most important relationships of my life.

4

TEENAGE KICKS

After that first night, I was desperate to go out again. I wanted my next fix of Stella. I wanted to get up to more mischief. For a few days I didn't hear from her. And then all of a sudden she started ringing me up and inviting me out.

And I became her little protégée. She knew everyone; she was a big face back then. And she took me everywhere with her, introduced me to a lot of people, opened my eyes to a lot of things, became my guide into a whole way of life. Obviously, a lot of them were the wrong places, and the wrong people, and the things she taught me I probably shouldn't have known about. I loved it.

At first, while I was still working for my dad's businesses, I only saw her every few weeks. The rest of the time I just carried on going out with my mum, looked forward to those Monday nights at the British Legion when I never had to pay a penny for my drinks, and the Tuesdays afterwards when

Mum's phone rang like a hotline all day (which wasn't a good thing in her eyes).

But then after my dad left, and I didn't have a job any more, my life fell into a new kind of pattern, all revolving around going out and about with Stella.

My mum didn't really have any control over me. To be honest I'm not sure she even tried. She was still quite young herself and she turned a blind eye because she liked going out with Stella too. And my dad wasn't around. When he did meet Stella, he couldn't stand her. First time he met her, he said, 'She's covered in perfume. That's to hide a different smell.' He couldn't understand why I would want to be going round with someone the same age as him. But first he was in prison, then he wasn't there at all. So he didn't really have anything to do with it.

School had given up on me by then too. I did actually make it into the exam room for my first O-level exam. Walked in and sat down in the hall with all the others with the paper in front of me. But then I just got up, turned my back, walked away, and never went back.

I wanted to do what I wanted to do, and no one was going to stop me.

I moved out from living with my mum and got my own little rented bedsit in Havering-atte-Bower. But I started spending most of my time at Stella's place, her little three-bed terrace on Manor Road in Romford. That became base camp for me, every Friday to Sunday, and soon on Wednesdays too. There was always something going on there, always a crowd. Even if you went round on a Sunday night she'd be sitting round the table with six well-known men, playing this card game – kalooki – for money.

A typical weekend, I'd get ready over at Stel's on a Friday evening. I had skintight dresses with net fishtails, and skirts that got shorter and shorter, and my handmade stiletto shoes. When I was seventeen, I got a fox fur jacket – blue fox cape with all fox tails hanging off it, from Leroy Furs in Romford. They were the in thing, and the more elaborate the better. My hair would be either a huge blonde permed hairdo that you couldn't get a comb near, or else I'd get the hair-dresser to put it back in a French plait. I wanted to make an impression when I walked in anywhere, and I did. People were so amazed to see someone so young done up so nice, rumours even started going round that my dad was a mil-lionaire. Load of old crap – it just shows you how Chinese whispers start.

And Stella – well, Stella looked all the ticket too. She was big built – not fat, but tall, with a nice figure, and she always wore very high shoes to make her even taller, full make-up, wigs, skirts with splits up them, fishnet tights. Trashy glitzy clothes. You'd look at her and think, My God, what is that? Once seen, never forgot. She wasn't one of them that wants to blend in with the crowd – she wanted to walk in and make a statement.

Then we'd head out. We got so we had all our own little haunts, and we became known at all of them. We'd hang out with everyone, different types of people in different places. And wherever it was, everywhere we went, I'd have blokes all over me.

We'd go to a pub or a club somewhere first. Me, Stella,

sometimes my mum, sometimes my Auntie Janet after she got divorced, sometimes others too. The Ilford Palais, with the coppers and the firemen in the doubles bar, the VIP bit. Or there was a club in Stratford we used to go to a lot, where a lot of bad boys used to hang out, bank robbers and that. Or the Circus Tavern. Or Palms, in Romford, which was a well-known cattle market full of sleazy older blokes looking for younger girls. I'd be out on the dance floor, strutting my stuff – disco, rock 'n' roll, jive, whatever – with everyone looking.

At chucking-out time, we'd drive to a steakhouse that was open after hours, the Dallas Steak House on the Hackney Road, where you could carry on drinking.

And then when we came out of the steakhouse, three o'clock in the morning, we'd head somewhere else, with Stella driving.

Stella drove everywhere. She stopped working for Jim Whybrew because they had a big falling out, lovers' tiff, and she started working for his son-in-law, doing the same thing, making mega-money – £500 a week, cash – and she always had a brand-new company car, better and better every year. First it was a brand-new Merc. And then in the end she got a Bentley. She loved that, because it was so flash. It was a talking point – one of her pulling things. Specially when she got her personalised number plate put on: 69 JOB.

She used to drink and drive – she'd drive on a bottle of vodka. But most of the time when she got pulled up, she'd blag it, talk her way round it. Sometimes they didn't even bother breathalysing her.

So we'd pile in the car – so many of us squashed into the

car – and Stella would take us to a private members' club, Ferdenzes, in Mayfair near the Ritz Hotel, that stayed open late for the rich Arabs and croupiers and working girls. The men used to want me to go on holiday with them. Or she'd take us to a club where women danced with snakes and some of the big East End crooks used to hang out, like Freddie Foreman and John Bindon. Or to a casino. Stella was a casino freak, used to play blackjack and she was very good at it. She taught me how to play but she wouldn't let me sit with her. 'Go away, you'll change me luck.' I'd have to sit on another table. But she'd let me go in on her playing money and then we'd split whatever she won.

Stella had gone out with Roy Shaw, the prizefighter, too, when she was younger. I think she'd even been engaged to him for fifteen minutes, and they'd remained friends. He was still feared everywhere he went, and if he was ever there when we walked in anywhere, we'd be straight into his company.

When the late clubs closed, we'd go on to the Early House, which was a pub in the East End somewhere – Bow, I think – that opened at six o'clock in the morning for the men working on the fish markets and the fruit markets and the train drivers coming off their shifts. It was just a rotten grotty blokes' pub really. The men would be sitting having a pint and a chat, six o'clock in the morning, and we'd barge in there, and Stella would make her entrance.

'Come on, everybody!' she'd scream.

'Oh, here she comes,' they'd all groan. Or they'd sing her theme tune: 'There could be trouble ahead.' And then she'd challenge them to a beer race – Stella had this thing where she could open up her throat and do a whole pint of bitter in two seconds – or start playing pool, tits hanging all over the table. We'd stay there until nine in the morning, and then go on somewhere else, when the normal pubs opened.

We'd keep going all day and then go out again Saturday night, do the same thing all over again.

And Stella, she just created mayhem wherever she went. If something was ever boring, she would disrupt it. If there was nothing going on, she would make things happen. She had the mentality of an eighteen-year-old really, just wanted to get up to mischief.

Like, she used to get out of her car at traffic lights, walk to the back of her motor, pull a different outfit out of the boot, and get changed right there in the road.

Or one night we kidnapped this life-size cardboard cut-out of a bloke holding a beer, from a display, and took it round with us all night. We cut a hole where its mouth was and stuck a fag in there, and Stella kept lighting it up. And of course it attracted attention, people would come over and go, 'What's all that about then?' Then they'd be caught in her circle.

Or if she got bored, she'd do a headstand, in the middle of a pub. In a very short skirt. Or draw on some bloke's face with a pen. That was her way.

So really, the bad boys, we could smell them out, and they could smell us out. We'd walk in, all loud and full-on, and they'd be straight over, and like, 'Oh we'll get this.' And the party would start. I could be out whole weekends and spend nothing at all. Just pay to get into places, and then the blokes would buy drinks for me and Stella all night. We looked like the bee's knees, and we were out there, and everyone knew us, and we attracted loads of attention wherever we went. And the more attention we got, the more comments we got, the more blokes in our circle, the more I liked it.

Going out on those Friday nights that went on all weekend was like being led on a big adventure by the most exciting person you could imagine. I never knew where I'd end up, or what I'd end up doing, but I knew it was going to be wild.

I thought Stella was a god. She was giving me a taste of the high life. Clubs, pubs, casinos, blokes.

Plus, I was seeing things, doing things, that normal teenagers didn't see or do. Petty stuff, and proper villain stuff too. Once the men trusted you, they talked like you weren't there. Cloning vehicles, money laundering, forging money, hijacking lorries. And Stella could get any problem sorted, anything at all – smooth things over, hide things that needed hiding, get people out the country. She had a really quick brain and nothing fazed her. I was like a sponge, taking it all in, who everyone was, how everything worked, all the different ways to earn quick money.

For Stella, I think at first she liked the way I attracted all the blokes. Because once the blokes had come over, then Stella would start up doing her thing – writing on their faces or whatever, having a laugh with them and getting everyone into her circle. But I think as well, that she saw me as a younger version of her, that she could mould. She did have a daughter, Denise, but in some ways I think I was more a daughter to her than Denise was.

*

There was a lot of speed about. This flash girl in our crowd used to buy it by the ounce, first thing when she got paid on a Friday, take a big bag of it everywhere we went. She was buying her way in I suppose. And you couldn't keep up unless you were speeding. There was just no way. Because sometimes from Friday night to Monday morning, you didn't sleep.

So when we were all out, and everyone was screaming, 'Come on, medication time!', I would get a bit of fast tipped off a false red fingernail and into my drink, like everyone else. Everyone had to take it or you just weren't on the right wavelength.

Then, within the hour, after you've taken it, your heart starts beating really quickly, your eyes go massive, really dilated, and you start talking a lot, talking a load of shit. And you start rushing around, you want to dance, you're really hyper, you've got to be moving all the time. Everything happens quicker than real life. Housewives take it to help them do all the housework. You lick your lips a lot too, and you move your jaw around, and you're thirsty, you just want to keep drinking and drinking. Five drinks to every one you'd normally have, so you're weeing all the time. And about ten hours later you come down, and you have to take another quarter of a gram. Probably over a weekend, I'd take three lots.

Some of the crowd used it for slimming too, because you don't eat at all when you're speeding, you can't eat. Sometimes I'd go out on a Friday and by the time I got home on a Sunday my jeans were so loose they were falling off.

But even speeding, I couldn't keep up with Stella. I've

never met anyone so hardcore. I've been out with her for three days without sleeping, and in the end I've had to give in before her. 'Can you take me home, I can't keep up. Another thing of whizz is not going to help me. I just can't do it anymore – it's not doing anything, just drop me home, please!' And the next morning she'd tell me about what she'd done after she dropped me home. The only thing that ever stopped Stella was if a nail fell off. That was the end of the world then – she couldn't go in anywhere without a nail on, and everything had to stop while she glued it back on. A nail fell off, it was all over!

So that's how it went, from when I was about seventeen to when I was twenty. Out on the town. It's all a bit of a blur now.

I did have a few little jobs through those years. I tried working in the farm shop after my dad sold it, but I couldn't work for someone there when I'd been used to running it myself. That lasted about three weeks. Sometimes I'd work stacking shelves in the newsagents where my mum had got herself a job. I done cleaning jobs. Cashier in a petrol garage. And one winter I got a job in a shop called Bambers in Romford, which was a women's clothes shop. I was salesperson of the month there. I was put in the coat department, which no one wanted because these coats were so expensive they were hard to sell. But I'd sell them. 'Oh, that looks lovely on you' – and all that. And I would keep walking up to the counter with another sale and another one, no one could believe it. But the manageress there, she was a right know-it-all and we didn't see eye to eye. I stuck it from

October to Christmas and then after Christmas I didn't go back.

I suppose I didn't have the best attitude. In my mind, I'd always been going to be my own boss. I wasn't good at working for anyone else. Tried it, didn't like it.

And after a bit, I was partying so hard that I couldn't have held down a legit job even if I'd wanted one, which I admit I didn't. Everything I've ever done, I've done to the best of my ability and that includes going out and getting wasted. And the thing about speed is, it gives you loads of energy, you can drink and drink and drink and keep going all night. But then afterwards you feel really terrible, like shit, for a couple of days. And I was going out Friday to Sunday, and then again on Wednesday. If I wanted the high life with Stella – and I did – I couldn't work.

So from the age of about seventeen I started doing this and that to make ends meet. Me and a couple of girls I met down the pub. Anything really. We started off selling stuff out of the back of a van. One of the girls, Vicky, some friends of her dad used to have warehouses, and she used to buy stuff cheap from them and then we'd go to packing companies and factories in Harold Hill on a Friday when people had just got paid and sell it.

And then I discovered kiting, and got quite good at it. That's chequebook fraud. You get someone's stolen cheque-book and you go into a Sainsbury's and buy £50 worth of cigarettes on it – because the cheque guarantee card is valid up to £50. Then you go to another supermarket and do it again, until you've used all the cheques. People used to sell the chequebooks and cards to us for £100, when they'd stolen a car with a handbag in it or something. We got two or three cartons of fags on each cheque, came back with a bootful of fags and sold them to the local newsagents.

Or we'd offer to do someone's shopping for them, some old biddy. And we would do it, too, we wouldn't rip them off. They'd write their list, we'd go in and get everything they put on it – they'd give us £50 for it. We'd pocket the £50 cash and use the stolen cheque card, and we'd get cash back at the till as well.

When the cheques ran out, we still had the card. No chip and PIN in those days. Most shops had certain limits where you could spend that much on the card and they wouldn't ring it through. We'd find out what the limits were. Or we'd go in with the shop owner against the bank. We'd get fifty quid's worth of stock, they'd ring it up for a hundred quid. The bank guaranteed them the money, so they'd make fifty quid out of it and we'd get the stock. Petrol stations used to do that too.

And shoplifting. We used to go into B&Q or Homebase and get one of those flat trolleys and lift power tools. Really expensive drills worth £100. Or the gold-plated taps, £150 a set. We'd buy something, but we'd hide the tools and the taps on the bottom of the trolley. We would go for the divvyest-looking person on the tills, the one that looked a bit not with it, keep them talking, distract them. Just wheel it through. Then sell it all on at half price to anyone we could find – mostly mates of my uncle's who worked for Radio Rentals. Or even take it back the next day and say we'd lost the receipt and get our full money back. They got wise to it in the end and one day we found the power tools weren't in the boxes anymore.

They're wise to all the tricks now, you'd never get away with that kind of thing these days, and they've got chip and PIN, but in them days it was quite easy.

One of the girls I was doing it with, Leeanne, she met a bloke called Dom, who was a lot older than her. He was tall and distinguished-looking with really nice clothes. We got chatting to him in the pub and it transpired that he was a professional kiter, that was his game. He had a little gang working for him, four or five people, and he used to drive them round to different towns and send them all out for the day using cards and chequebooks. He knew all the best places to do it everywhere he went. Before we knew it, Leeanne was seeing him and I was part of his gang. He would take us to Clacton for the weekend, put us up in a caravan site, Butlins or Warners, and we'd all go out kiting.

I even went international. My brother Gary was living out in Tenerife for a while getting over a break-up with a girlfriend. I heard he had no money and I felt sorry for him. I went out to visit and took lots of chequebooks with me. There were loads of people out there who wanted to buy them off me, and it was so easy to use them. We lived like millionaires on these cards that weren't ours.

I got a real buzz out of it, getting something for nothing.

The other thing I did for money was I sometimes pretended to be Stella's assistant, at her work. I used to go out to meetings with her and stay in hotels all on the company. I remember I'd be sitting in these meetings and they'd be asking me questions and I used to have to blag it. Or we'd be in some warehouse and she'd make me climb up a load of pallets, just to make it look good and give her a laugh. 'Oh,

Trace, could you climb up and count them for me, please?' I even worked as her chauffeur for a bit when she got done for drink driving and lost her licence.

One time we were driving back from one of these meetings, down the motorway from Birmingham. We were in Stella's white Merc, with the personalised number plate, and she'd pulled the blind down at the back that said 'Beep if you want a bonk'. It was a really hot day and we decided we were going to drive along with me topless, and her bottomless. She was driving her Mercedes at a hundred miles an hour down the motorway, with both of us half naked. Lorries were nearly crashing. And then this one bloke in a car started to race us. He went faster, we went faster. He went faster, we went faster. In the end he couldn't get the better of her and he pulled her over. He said to us, 'I done everything to get past you. I haven't ever seen a driver like you in my life.' He owned a string of sunbed shops and a four-storey nightclub in Birmingham with a casino next door, and he invited us to come as his guests. We went there quite regularly after that, and because he was paying we always used to drink pink Cristal champagne.

And then it just made sense really for me to start selling a bit of speed. Everyone in our circle was taking it, because you couldn't keep up otherwise.

Stella introduced me to someone who manufactured it – speed's a man-made drug – and I used to buy it in bulk from him, a kilo at a time. I couldn't store it in my bedsit because it smelt of cat's piss. Have it inside for an hour and the place would reek of it. So I would store it in my mum's shed, or her

garage, or in her freezer, wrapped in a brown bag. I wasn't
dealing on the streets; I only needed to deal to quite a small
circle, and that gave me a nice steady income.

At first, I was just selling it in wraps, £15 a gram. But as
time moved on, I started selling it in ounces. I'd buy the kilo
for £2000 and cut it with glucose powder or vitamin powder,
anything powdery with a bland taste, to make that into
maybe a kilo and a half, or two kilos. So I'd have seventy
ounces, and I'd sell that at £120 an ounce to four or five
people a week over maybe three months and make £200 or
£300 a week. Regular income, without having to do anything,
and I could still go out with Stella.

By the age of twenty I had got myself a bit of a record. Never
for anything major.

First I got done for smashing up a car – criminal damage.
I was at a party and one of our neighbours, a nuisance neighbour from our street, came up to me and my brother, really
drunk. He was goading me and Gary, saying over and over
again, 'You think you own this street.' He wouldn't go away
and we got rowing and then he left the party. When we got
back to my mum's house, we saw him on the street and we
went over there. 'You was all right starting in the house – let's
see how good you are now.' My mum was out in the street,
screaming: 'Come on, come on.' We'd all been drinking. I
ended up putting a brick through the back window of his car.
I got a year's probation for that.

Then when I was about eighteen, I got done for one ounce
of speed. I'd taken something, and it must have been bad
because I started hallucinating. I was running around in the

road and the police were called and I got nicked because there was fast in my handbag. It was when I was on bail for that that I decided to go out to Tenerife to see my brother. So then, when I got back, months later, there was a warrant out for me and I had to go and hand myself in at the local police station. Judge at Snaresbrook County Court gave me eighteen months probation and a fine.

And then I got caught kiting. I was in a shop in Upminster and I'd bought something on a stolen card and I'd asked for cash back. There was some query on the signature and the girl behind the counter started doing some checks. I ran off but she must have rung the police because I got caught running up the road and taken to Romford police station. I got fined for that one.

In the meantime, my brother Gary, two years younger than me, went off to become an apprentice in block paving when he was sixteen. He worked hard and never got in trouble. If he had a problem he came to me and I sorted it out. Fought his battles for him – literally, beat people up for him, bailed him out when he needed money.

Everybody loved him, and no one could ever believe he had a sister like me.

Chapter 5

GYPSY WOMAN

I was with a lot of bad boys in my life, but Chopper's Charlie was probably the baddest of them all.

I used to get loads of attention from all the blokes, had them all over me. I could pull anything I wanted. And I had an eye for a bad boy, could never have a boring bloke – which has got me into a lot of trouble over the years. So there was blokes, yes, but there was never anyone serious, because I wanted to go about town with Stella all the time.

My very first boyfriend, before I even met Stella, was Johnnie Fenton. That's who I lost my virginity to. I was about sixteen, and he was about eighteen. After a bit he used to stay at our house overnight, which was fine because by that point my dad wasn't there, he was in prison. That lasted about a year, and then he left me for someone else.

Billy Turner was next. I was quite taken with him, he was lovely. He was a motorbike racer; he had a scrambler and did competitive racing on it, and his mum and dad had a big house with a swimming pool in Collier Row. One day this Billy Turner came into the farm shop where I was working and I thought, Mmmmmm! I really liked the look of him. He went to my friend Rob's school, so I asked Rob to have a word with him, and the next day he rang me up and invited me out. We were together maybe seven or eight months.

But then as I met more and more people, when I was out and about with Stella, Billy started to seem a bit amateurish to me. I wanted to go on to bigger and better things and I dropped Billy and started up with Darren Adams, one of them Adams brothers, the ones who used to flash the cash about at singles nights. I wasn't with him, exactly, but every Friday night we used to end up together. It was one of them kind of things.

I met my first gypsy when I was out with Stella one night. He was a few years older than me and working as a tree feller with his dad, and he used to pick me up from my mum's house every night and take me out in his car. Name of Joey Drake. Macho man, boxer, with a really pretty face. I think he was probably my first love, I was pretty taken with him. But he was unlucky, because he came to get me on one of the rare times my dad came round the house after he was out of prison and he'd left us, and my dad went out the house and grabbed him by the throat, had him over the bonnet of his motor. He was shouting, 'She's still at school!!!!!' Even though I weren't. So that was the end of that relationship.

I did get myself a bit of a taste for gypsies though. To me, they were different, and dangerous. It seemed like they had no morals, no rules – they just did what they wanted to do. Law unto themselves. The way they earned their living, even the way they talked, was different. My ones were very handsome too.

And then there was Kevin Carter, from the Inter City Firm, who were really bad West Ham football hooligans. I met him out in Tenerife.

There was lots of others, to be honest. Some were just the one night, some a few months, on and off. If I saw someone I liked the look of, I would say 'See him, I'm having him.' I always did too.

I never ever left Stella to go off with a bloke though. I used to take them back to Stella's house and the party would carry on there. More booze, more gear, and then back out again, up to no good. Speed doesn't do much for your sex drive anyway.

I don't regret those blokes. I do bitterly regret that I didn't take more precautions though. Because I ended up, through my early twenties, having a couple of abortions. And although I can convince myself that those babies were better off not being born – because I would have made a terrible mother back then, and the men would have made even worse fathers, and they would have been exactly the kind of kids that end up off the rails and in prison – it does still hurt, and I do still beat myself up about it.

The first one was a baby that I'd planned on keeping at first. It was Kevin Carter's baby so I was about twenty-one. We'd shacked up together when we'd got back from Tenerife and found out I was pregnant. But he was a football hooligan and a puff head who just wanted to live off me, and one day we had a big row about the fact that he was doing nothing all day – if he was like that now, what was he going to be like when the baby came? – and he walked out. I just couldn't think how I was going to be able to bring this kid up on my own, so I rang the clinic in Buckhurst Hill and booked in for an abortion. My brother Gary paid for it, and he took me there. But when I came round from the anaesthetic, I was still pregnant. 'You're too far gone, my dear,' the doctor said. I was much further than I thought I was – eighteen weeks – and that was too late for this clinic. So I was going to have to go and do it all again at a different clinic in London the next day – on the train, on my own. I very nearly didn't go. I didn't really want to. But my mum, and my brother, were saying I wouldn't be able to make it on my own with this kid. 'Tracy, you can't bring that baby up, you've got to do this.'

I saw women at that clinic who were really far gone. They were going to have to be induced and give birth to the babies they were aborting. Luckily I was just early enough not to have to do that; they put me under and did it that way.

After that at least I had them early – at six weeks – as early as I knew I was pregnant. One was by a bloke called Danny Tyler, and the other I don't think I ever knew whose it was.

Everything I do, I do to the maximum. To the extreme. So in my business now, when I make sausage, it's got to be the best sausage, and the most flavours. And back when I was mixing with bad boys, I had to fall in love with the very baddest one about.

When I was about twenty-one, I started hearing talk about a new gypsy who'd moved onto the site in Rush Green, called Chopper's Charlie. All the talk was about how he dressed really smart, and how he drove a really flash car, and how he had loads of money. And about his violent temper and what he'd done. Charlie must have been about forty years old when I met him, and he had just finished a really long prison sentence.

He'd got about twelve years for what he'd done, but he'd caused so much trouble in prison they'd kept adding on years, so he'd done more like fifteen years in all, a lot of it in solitary. Charlie had come to be living on the site in Rush Green because he'd followed a woman to Romford. Word was, he'd wasted no time establishing himself on that site and in the town. Every site needs someone who's in charge – someone forceful who's going to intimidate all the others, so they can keep a bit of control and make sure not just anyone pulls into the site. Like on *My Big Fat Gypsy Wedding*, it was Paddy Doherty, who went on *Big Brother*. Well, Charlie made sure the man in charge was him. It helped that he had relatives on the site who'd spent years spreading the word of what a psycho nutcase he was. He chucked off the people he didn't want there, put his horses on the council-owned field, built stables at the back on the council-owned land, parked his lorries up wherever he wanted, even on other people's plots. Took the best pitch for himself, threw another family off there. He just done what he wanted, he ruled the roost. And in town, in the pubs and nightclubs, if anyone said something the wrong way to him once, you could be sure they wouldn't ever get it wrong again.

So you can imagine everybody was talking about Charlie. And you can imagine what they were saying. This was a really bad boy. Everyone knew him, everyone was petrified of him – he was the gypsy no one wanted to fight. But that was the attraction for me really. I had to meet him.

It was a Sunday night, and I walked into this pub in Romford. I knew he'd be there, because his car was parked on the pavement right outside – brand-new, top-of-the-range silver Escort RS, fully skirted, only two in the country, you couldn't miss it. And there he was. Ugly, really ugly, ugly as sin. Skin like orange peel, and teeth missing, and a nose that had been broken lots of times. But there was something about him. He was very smart, with tailored suit trousers and a really nice cardigan, and expensive-looking shoes. I could tell he'd spent a lot of money on his clothes. And he had these really piercing blue eyes, the bluest eyes you've ever seen, that looked at you and just, I don't know, just done it, I really loved them. He wasn't tall, but he was really muscly and strong on his top half, like people are when they've spent a lot of time in prison doing weights. You could tell he didn't give a shit for nothing or no one.

So I went up to him and he knew my dad – he and my dad had done bits and pieces together years ago. And that broke the ice.

He picked me up the next day from my mum's house and took me to a steakhouse down Romford Road. He was quite well known there, he'd already been putting himself about, so it was all 'Hello, Charlie, sir' and that, all respectful.

That night, he let me see how he had thousands of

pounds in cash in his pocket. He told me how he spent £1000 a time at BaronJon's, on designer clothes, how they all thought it was Christmas when he turned up there.

The campaign went on for about two weeks.

He wined and dined me. Everywhere he went he had a crowd of people round him. He was buying big rounds of drinks, playing cards, spinning the coin. Spinning the coin is where you toss a coin up in the air and you have to guess whether it's heads or tails. Only they would be doing it for £1000 a spin. I found out later that he had a coin with two heads on. Other people probably knew too, but they were too scared to argue. He even raced his horse down the A127 one Sunday morning – the police had to shut the whole road off because these two gypsies were riding their horses down the road.

He took me to see the site and I liked it. It was obvious, too, that he was the main man there. The council owned the site, but you would have thought he did; you had to ask him if you wanted to move on there. And usually the answer was no. 'No, there's no room. Ta ta.' It suited Charlie, and it suited the council. And it suited me; I was well impressed.

He took me to meet his mum and some of his fourteen brothers and sisters. They were all called 'Chopper's' after their dad. He was called Chopper, and they were his, so they were Chopper's Steve, Chopper's John and all that. Chopper himself put me on edge a bit and so did some of the sisters. But the mum was very quiet, a real old-fashioned gypsy woman, sat there like a queen bee while they all paid their respects to her. She had grey hair, greased into a long plait down her back, and a worn face; you could see she'd had a hard life.

He even got his teeth fixed.

People did warn me. They told me he had a temper on him and that's why his last woman had left him. They told me other women had left him because of it too.

So I had been told. But I thought it wasn't going to be like that for me. I thought it couldn't be the same bloke; he must have changed because he seemed so nice. Talk about honeymoon period. I was completely taken with him, smitten.

I moved in with him, into his mobile home on the site in Rush Green. At which point, everything changed.

Chapter 6

STIR CRAZY

Once I'd moved in with Charlie, I had to do the gypsy life, and do it Charlie's way. That meant all I did was clean, all day. Clean, and cook. My job as a gypsy wife was to feed him, and to clean, clean, clean.

At first, I liked it. And looking back, it's obvious now that for the first couple of weeks he was just settling me in.

The site itself was just by a big fishing lake in Rush Green. It had about sixteen families living on it, sixteen plots, running on both sides of a central path. A few families still had lots of children, elevens and thirteens, but most had moved with the times and just had twos and threes. The women had names like Alice and Rose, names that have come back in now but sounded old-fashioned back then.

Each mobile home had its own pitch, with a shed outside each one for a washing machine, a tumble dryer, a shower, a big basin, and a toilet. The mobile homes did have toilets in them, but most gypsies wouldn't use them, they considered that unhealthy. You live in it, you don't use the toilet. Even if you got up in the middle of the night you had to go outside but that didn't really bother me. I'd go late at night and hope I wouldn't need to go again until the morning.

Charlie had a double pitch, and the best mobile home, top of the range. It was really lovely, not like you'd think a mobile home would be at all. Three bedrooms – one for us, one for our clothes and one just spare – a bath, fitted kitchen, two leather chesterfield sofas, luxury fitted Sultana carpet, £20 a metre with pink swirls, and real lace curtains £150 a throw. He had really expensive artificial flowers in vases, and at least fifty grand's worth of Crown Derby china – teapots and dinner services and that – and it was all out on display in there, because that was their way. The china was their currency – they would swap it with each other, use it to buy horses – it was how you showed your wealth. Any traveller could have walked into his caravan and they would know how much the china was worth and how much the lace had cost.

I'm quite a good cook, and I enjoy it. Charlie taught me how to make the things he liked – fresh sausage rolls, and stews, and meat pudding, which is a traditional gypsy dish made out of suet. He liked a steak and kidney meat pudding. You roll the suet out, like pastry, and put all your meat and your onions in it, and then you wrap up the lot like a parcel, put it in a mutton cloth and tie it round with string, and boil it for four hours. Then when it's done you open it up, cut the top off, and pour gravy in. It tasted beautiful. And I already knew how to make lasagne and shepherd's pie.

And I baked: fairy cakes, lemon meringues – he'd always have a dessert.

So every day I would get up, make him two cups of tea and his breakfast, and then he would go out and mess with his horses. He'd be gone for an hour or so and then he'd come back and I'd make him another cup of tea. He'd open the door and go, 'TEA!' and I'd make it in a teapot using real tea-leaves and he'd drink it out of a bone china teacup. Off for another couple of hours, back for another cup of tea and a sausage roll, then another couple of hours and a cup of tea and lunch. He'd get me fresh bread every day that I had to slice and he'd have it with ham and cheese or something like that. More tea and a cake in the afternoon. By four o'clock he'd be back for the day, and I'd be done with all my cleaning: the washing and the ironing would be done, the pitch would be swept and hosed down, and the place would be immaculate with all the china spotless and gleaming. We'd sit watching wildlife programmes on the telly and having a laugh.

So, at first, I didn't mind that my world had shrunk to one person in one caravan on one site, I didn't mind the little rut he kept me in. I liked the routine and the feeling that I didn't have to worry about anything. I wasn't having to fend for myself, think about where my money was going to come from, what scam I was going to pull off next; I could be calm and relaxed.

And me and Charlie, together in our little world, we got on quite well, we understood each other.

But Charlie was a real old-fashioned gypsy. The way he'd been brought up, women had to keep in their place, and I guess because of those years in prison he hadn't moved with the times. I was his possession, I belonged to him, so he decided what I could do, what I could wear, and who I could talk to.

I wasn't allowed out, I wasn't allowed to see my friends, I had to forget about all of that. He said he was all I needed. My mum was allowed to visit sometimes, but he didn't really like that either. Because she was still going out and about, he would say that she was trying to brainwash me into leaving him and going back out on the town. He wouldn't let me talk to her on my own – he would always have to be there.

He bought me all new clothes – my old ones he told me not to bother bringing with me. Money was no object, he didn't mind what I spent, I could have a £300 jumper if I wanted it. But the skirts had to be at least twenty-nine inches, they had to be below the knee, and my tops couldn't show any flesh at all. I got mostly jogging bottoms and baggy T-shirts for doing the cleaning, and a few nice things for if we ever went out to visit his mum. His good clothes, the ones I'd been so impressed with, all got locked away and he just wore his old work clothes.

There was no going out anymore. Occasionally we might go out for dinner, just the two of us. But there was no more pubs. He didn't see the point of it now that I was there with him. And no alcohol at all, for him or for me.

And if there was a man at the door I was allowed to answer it, but I had to just say where he was and then walk away and shut the door up.

I wasn't even allowed to talk to the other women on the

site. He didn't want them gossiping and telling me things. That wasn't to do with the gypsy lifestyle, that was to do with Charlie. Lots of the other gypsies thought nothing of letting their wives sit with loads of people. In fact most of the women on the site were all very cliquey together. A lot of them were cousins anyway, and they had a system where they would all clean the caravans together. They'd all clean one, then all go to the next one and clean that, and then they'd sit together in each other's caravans when they'd finished. I was definitely not allowed in that gang.

One day, when Charlie was out with his horses, there was a knock at the door. It was Sarah, not even a friend, but someone I knew and he knew. She'd come onto the site to visit someone else and had heard I was there. I let her in for a cup of tea. When Charlie came back and saw her there, he didn't say anything in front of her, but I could tell he wasn't happy.

Sarah felt the atmosphere and left pretty quickly. She probably knew she shouldn't have been there, because she knew Charlie. I never even saw it coming. I clocked Charlie sitting there with no expression on his face. Then he said, 'Come out in the kitchen,' and I followed him in there. He said 'Don't. Ever.' And then he just lost it.

I didn't even think about trying to stop him. I didn't want to provoke him anymore.

After a bit I cleaned everything up, put the kettle on, and joined Charlie on the sofa. 'See what you made me do?' he said. 'See what you made me do?'

*

I tried really really hard, because I really did love him. And in a way, I quite liked the life. I got into a system, a routine, my whole day was mapped out for me. I liked seeing everything spotless. And I was being taken care of.

And it wasn't even the temper. I could take that. But I was getting stir crazy for my old life, I still wanted that too.

So I decided I was going to run away. It took a lot of planning. The only time I was allowed out on my own was on a Saturday, for an hour, to do the shopping at the local Rush Green parade of shops. I was allowed to go to Somerfield to do the big shop, and then the butcher's, and the baker's, and maybe the chemist's if I needed anything there. Just those four places, and I had to get everything I was going to need for the whole week. And the car had to be parked on the pavement outside Somerfield so that if he walked past – which he did – he would know I was there.

But on Sundays I knew Charlie would always be out all day. He went out trotting his horse in the morning, every Sunday, religiously, and in the afternoon he would usually go and do spin the coin to earn some money down the pubs. Even if he didn't go to the pubs, he still wouldn't be back until three o'clock, so I knew I had five hours.

My mum used to ring me on Sundays, when he wasn't there. I told her to get my brother Gary to pick me up from the site entrance the next Sunday.

The Sunday came and I felt sick. He trotted his horses every Sunday, but what if he didn't this Sunday? He never got back early, but what if he got back early just this time? Plus, I didn't have a suitcase so I was going to have to put everything in black bags and carry them through the site.

There were no mobile phones then so even if someone saw me there was no way they could tell him. But I felt sick thinking about it.

I did it though. I carried my bags through the site and I put them in Gary's car and he drove me away.

I'd given up my little bedsit when I'd moved in with Charlie – I had thought I wasn't going to need it and anyway I couldn't afford to keep it on because Charlie wouldn't let me sign on. So I had to go back to my mum's. When I got there, back to the house where I'd grown up, on the estate in Harold Wood, it was just a feeling of relief. I'd made it to safety. But Mum didn't want me in the house. She knew Charlie, and she was scared of him. I didn't know what to do – I had nowhere to go. So I went to Stella's – she wasn't scared of anyone – and she took me in.

The next day, I was gutted I'd done it. But I knew I couldn't go back on the site; in his eyes that would be disrespecting him even more and I couldn't afford to do that.

For a while I just lay low, and stayed inside at Stella's. But after a few weeks I thought it would be all right to venture back into Romford. At first, into places I knew he wouldn't go. And then I started to get braver. I was out one night, in the Res nightclub. It was the pisshole of the world this place, grimy and dirty, a disco in a basement, the kind of place that when you came out you'd have drink slopped all down your legs. But everyone loved it, because you could do what you liked in there and it went on until three o'clock in the morning.

And I was in there, all dolled up in a short skirt and a tight top, and I turned around, and he was there, on the other side of the dance floor. He looked straight at me with his eyes glinting and he started to walk over to me. When he was close enough for me to hear him, he just beckoned with his index finger. Slowly. 'Come here,' he growled, 'I want you.' I was too frightened not to. No one else was going to intervene in that, either. We walked out together, then he threw me in his car and took me back to the site.

He went mental when we got back. He was really out of control that time. But he told me he loved me, and I loved him too, no doubt about it. So I tried again.

We got back to all our routines. I got back to cleaning and cooking, to my little rut. Charlie bought me jewellery, big diamond rings, and thick gold chains with gold coins on them that weighed five ounces. And he took me to a shop his sisters all went to and bought me big bobbly handmade cardigans – far too good to do the cleaning in, and too heavy too because they were pure wool so it was like walking round with a coat on your back.

Sometimes I'd do something wrong and he'd lose his temper. Like one time he was in the bath and I answered the door. It was a man, so I should have just said he was in the bath, shut the door, and walked away. But after I'd said Charlie was in the bath this man said something to me, asked me, 'How are you?' or something like that. And I didn't walk away, I said something back to him, like, 'I'm fine, thank you.'

He'd go very quiet and still. Then his piercing blue eyes would go glittery and the whites of his eyes would go red and he'd smash something up. That's all it needed really. I wouldn't try to stop him or anything, there wasn't any point. And then afterwards he'd say, 'You made me do that, didn't ya?' And I'd start to think the same way as him, that I shouldn't have done that. I did make that mistake with the door more than once though.

I stuck it out for another few weeks, maybe a couple of months. And then things started playing on my mind again. I'd managed to use the phone a few times when he'd been out, always frightened that he would come back in and catch me. But now I was terrified about what would happen when the bill came. If any of the phone calls had been too long, they'd be itemised on the bill. I was living on my nerves.

If I was going to leave again, I had to do it right this time.

I started plotting it out. I had no money of my own so I had to try to nick pound coins whenever I could. He had a big jar on the table where he used to put all his change and if it got quite full I could take a few without him noticing. I hid them in the linen basket, under the washing.

I knew I couldn't take the clothes he'd bought me, or any of the jewellery. I knew that they were his, not mine, and if I'd taken any of it with me he would have hunted me down for it and made me pay. It was best to just leave it. And the stuff I'd taken with me the first time I'd run away, all my old clothes from my old life, I hadn't even bothered bringing those back. So I didn't have much to take this time.

I went to stay at Stella's again. Then one day I was at my mum's house – she was on edge me even being there, jumping at every little sound – and the phone went, and I picked it up. It was Charlie. He whispered, 'I'm gonna come round to your mum's house for you if you don't come back.'

So I walked down to the end of the road and he put me in his car again.

I kept on trying with Charlie, for about two years. It was agony. Agony when I was with him, and agony when I wasn't. I wanted it, and I didn't want it, if that makes sense.

We loved each other, and we really understood each other, we were on the same wavelength. There was a real connection there. When it was good, it was like we weren't a man and a woman, we were mates, and he would say I was much smarter than a normal woman. He would even admit I wasn't stupid, which was an amazing compliment from him because everyone was a div to him, or a fucking stupid prick. Everyone was beneath him, but he respected me; he never called me a div, and that meant a lot to me. When it was good, it was good as gold.

I would have done anything for him. I did do quite a lot. I knew all his little secrets about how he made his money, and I never told.

But I could have done much worse for him. I think I would have done anything he asked me to if he was in trouble, anything.

He tried his hardest for me, too. Like, after about eighteen months, he actually let a hairdresser come on site and highlight my hair, which was a really big thing. All the other gypsies on the site couldn't believe he'd allowed it. Maybe he'd noticed that every time my roots grew out I ran away.

I loved him, and he loved me, and I didn't have friends or family telling me I should get out of it. Stella never used to voice her opinion really – she's just someone who lets you get on with it. She might have sometimes said, 'What do you want to go back with that wanker for?' Or, 'It's his fucking loss, not yours.' But that was about it. My dad wasn't around. And my mum, she will admit, used to be relieved when I was back with Charlie, because she could sleep at night knowing where I was and that I wasn't out on the rampage or lying drunk in a ditch somewhere.

I used to go over it and over it in my mind, trying to think what was wrong with me, why I couldn't make it work. Trying to talk myself into believing I could do it. I really wanted to be with him. Why couldn't I change my ways and give up my life for him? It wasn't the temper. It was that I just couldn't cut myself off from the world. If he could have let me see my friends sometimes, I think I could have done it. Or even if I couldn't have seen my friends but I'd been allowed sometimes to get in the car and drive over to my mum's. I wasn't asking for the world, just normal things, but he couldn't allow it.

I wanted it. But I couldn't do it the way he had to have it. So time and again, after three or four months, I couldn't take it anymore, the boredom, and the loneliness, and I'd run away. I must have run away maybe ten times – I know I never made it longer than three or four months.

But every time I ran away, he'd eventually find me. Sometimes after a week, sometimes I'd be gone for months. He'd find me, and put me in the car, and I'd know what was coming.

When I got back, it would all be waiting there for me. The fifty grand's worth of Crown Derby china, and the clothes and the jewellery. And the ranting and raging. Sometimes he'd have that wild glint in his eye and it would be really bad, sometimes it would just be a few things got smashed up so people could see he hadn't just taken me back without doing anything. And then I'd put the clothes and the jewellery back on and we'd carry on as if I'd never been away. That's how it was. Every time.

And, because he really did love me, he kept taking me back. He told me that he loved me, and once he even said, 'You don't know how much you've hurt me. You broke my heart.' I don't think he's ever admitted that to anyone.

And I kept going back, because I loved him too, and I suppose I couldn't get him out of my system. Charlie was the love of my life. I still think of him fondly. I probably still love him now. But in the end, I just couldn't live that life with him. Thank God I never got pregnant because then I'd never have got away. And if I'd stayed with him I think I would have ended up in a mental institution ten years sooner than I did.

7

THE ONLY WAY IS MAGALUF!

By the time I left Chopper's Charlie for the last time, it had become a familiar routine. Walked out on a Sunday while Charlie was doing his horses, found a cab, went round to Stella's house. Only this time, when Stella let me in, like she always did, there were her suitcases all over the floor. All half-packed.

'What's going on here then?' I asked, a bit shocked. 'Where are you going?' It hadn't occurred to me that one day I could run away and Stella wouldn't be there waiting for me.

'Going to Spain,' she said, quite offhand. 'Going Tuesday.'

'Who with?' I wanted to know.

'Oh, my friend Sam, Sam Clark.' That was another surprise.

'Oh yeah.'

'Yeah. Me and Petey are going' – Petey was her little boy,

he was six now –'and Sam's taking her two boys, and Sam's mum's coming to look after the kids while we go out and that. Going for a fortnight.'

Well I knew of this Sam, I'd seen her with her husband in the pubs, but I didn't know her. I'd never had a conversation with her. I didn't like the sound of Stella going on holiday with this Sam.

'Oh,' I said.

'Why don't you come with us?' said Stella.

I brightened up. 'Can I? Yeah, I wouldn't mind.'

'Yeah.'

So I did. They were leaving on the Tuesday, so I spent Monday rushing round my mum's and the travel agents and that, getting some money together and sorting out a ticket on the same flight, and a seat on the same coach to Gatwick, the Gatwick Flyer. I didn't have any clothes to wear but I could buy them out there. And Stella was going to let me bunk with her in her hotel room. Our posse was so big and chaotic, she'd cause some kind of commotion in the lobby when we arrived and I'd sneak in without anyone noticing.

Only Stella didn't tell Sam about me coming.

We got on the coach first – me, Stella, her little boy Petey, and a friend's daughter, who Stella had brought along to babysit. The Flyer picked us up from Stella's house, and then it drove us round to Sam's place in Brentwood, a big house on the Brook Street roundabout. The coach pulled up, and two boys came out the house, Chris and Connor, identical twin boys around six years old, and then Sam's mum. Sam got busy loading all their gear into the luggage hold. And then she walked on the coach. We were the only ones on there. And Sam looked at me, and I suppose I looked back at her.

Sam wasn't over-the-top glamorous like me and Stella, she was more a mumsy type. She had a sensible hairdo – short and blow-dried. Nice figure, a size twelve then and always, and her face was pretty enough, but she was no striking beauty. She was six years older than me so she would have been about twenty-eight, twenty-nine years old.

'This is Tracy,' said Stella. 'Do you know Tracy?'

'Well sort of, yeah.'

'Well, she's coming with us.'

And I thought, Oh my God, she hasn't even had the decency to tell her.

It wasn't a good start. Frosty, you might say. Awkward. You could have cut it with a knife – on the coach, at the airport, on the plane to Palma, and all the way to the hotel. Put me in Sam's shoes, I probably would have been the same. Her nose was right out of joint and mine would have been too. I really felt for her.

I went to bed feeling like a right gooseberry and thinking I shouldn't have come. But the next morning Stella decided she had to hire a Jeep, and she sent me and Sam out to do it. That's all it took. We started having a laugh and a joke together while we were sorting out this Jeep hire and we found we had the same naughty sense of humour and we could really make each other laugh. Mostly taking the piss out of Stella and all her ailments, doing impressions of her moaning about her legs and that. Mean really, but funny. Plus she was obviously quite a naughty girl, Sam, and I liked that, I found it amusing. By the time we got back to the hotel, we'd bonded, a friendship had started.

It was a good job we did hit it off, too, because unbeknownst to both of us Stella had also invited her boss along. She'd been flirting with him and she had told him she was going to Magaluf and invited him to come. And the first we knew of this was about four days into the holiday, when we were all in Stella's hotel room at three o'clock in the morning and the phone went and it was this bloke, and off she rushed to Palma Airport to pick him up.

We were gobsmacked. We couldn't believe Stella had the audacity to invite this bloke along and not even tell us. And Stella and this bloke – we named him Tenko straight away because he used to wear these khaki army shorts – they disappeared into her bedroom for the rest of the week.

So it was just me and Sam, having a whale of a time, out and about, getting up to all sorts of mischief. And I thought I could relax because I knew Charlie would never find me in Spain. He didn't move in the same circle of friends as me – there was no one to tell him where I was. I was safe.

Magaluf in the summer of 1987 was a mental place. Steaming hot, and absolutely over the top. It was very English, with loads of pubs and bars on a big strip, and half-dressed girls outside, each one trying to entice you in with free drinks and that. Inside it would be half-price cocktails and everyone out in big groups of blokes, or big groups of girls, spewing up all over the place. I loved it.

Our hotel was right on the beach, about half an hour from Palma Airport, right in the heart of Magaluf. Palmanova I think it was called. It wasn't the best but it was one of the better ones in Magaluf, three or four star, and we had half board so all our breakfasts and evening meals were included. Stella's plan for all that had worked. Somehow I'd got into Stella's hotel room on the first day, and then because they'd seen me there from the beginning the hotel assumed I was legit, so I was eating all my meals there, morning and night. You wouldn't get away with it these days, but in those days you didn't have to wear armbands or anything, and we were all eating at different times anyway and they obviously just weren't keeping track of it all.

So on a normal evening, first we'd get all dressed up. With Sam it would always be short skirts, or shorts, because her legs were the best part of her and she knew it. She used to be a junior swimming champion when she was younger and had really good legs, they were perfect. With me, I bought my clothes out there at the market in Magaluf and at the time it was all brightly coloured shorts sets. Tight shorts and little matching tops, and I bought two or three in different colours. And a couple of tight-fitting dresses, clingy stuff that showed off my figure. All with high-heeled white stilettos.

We'd be quite sensible until about eight o'clock – we had to wait for Sam and Stella to do the motherly bits, take the kids out and feed them and that – and then the fun would begin. We'd start off in this one particular bar that did buy-one-get-one-free drinks, or half-price drinks, or even sometimes free drinks. This bar – it was Mano's bar I think – had a duck in it, a real duck, as a novelty factor. It would waddle out three or four times a night, chase the girls around the bar, bite their bums, and then get taken back behind the bar again. There would be a lot of squealing and screaming and laughing – a really good atmosphere, and everyone used to go there. I loved it – there was so many people, and I was right in the middle of the action.

Then we'd move on to another place, and another, and then there'd be particular places we'd end up at the end of the night. And at one o'clock in the morning, everyone would head to the clubs, and they'd go on till about six o'clock. We'd come out at six, get back to the hotel about seven or eight, just when the boys were getting up. Half the time, Sam would have to blag it and go and take her boys for breakfast, pretend she hadn't been out all night.

Obviously we had our speed with us. So some days I'd be speeding and just try to keep going and going. Others, I went to bed for a few hours, or tried to sleep it off round the swimming pool before it was time to get started again. You're powerful when you're young – you can just get on with it. I found the days quite mundane, I couldn't wait to get out. I wished it was night all the time.

So that was a normal night, but most of the nights weren't ever normal because something was always happening. Like for about four or five nights the navy was in port, 5000 American naval officers. These officers were allowed out at night to roam the town, with loads of money to spend, and they were rowdy and naughty and out of control. Well, me and Sam decided we was going to get to know them a bit better, give our eyes a treat. I was in my element. Millions of blokes – in uniform, which made it even better – drink flowing, me all dolled up and getting lots of attention, just giving it large all night until the Military Police came and rounded them all up. I don't think I spent any money on those nights.

Another night Sam was dancing on a table in a disco called BCM, and she fell off and smashed her head open, broke something too, maybe an ankle, and we had to take her to hospital.

The boys made their own mark on Magaluf. One day we were snoozing on sun loungers round the pool and we heard fire engines going past. We was laughing and joking about it but then the police turned up with guns. It turned out it was Sam's two boys – they'd started a fire in some dry grass round the back of some shops. The next day they set the curtains on fire in their bedroom. They were only young, but those boys were really naughty, and not just in Magaluf. At home, they'd been thrown out of schools; they'd pulled tiles off their mum's roof. Sam was pulling her hair out over them. They were trouble.

And I made a friend too. A little boxer from a big family in Shoreditch or maybe Mile End, that was staying at the hotel with his mates, name of Steven Trevisi. He was hanging around killing time, waiting to go to Camp America to teach boxing. And we came up with this idea to sell Stella's earache tablets in the nightclubs, make a bit of money. Stella was in on it too. The plan was, Stella would let me and Steve have the tablets, and we were going to sell all these tablets on the last day of the holiday and then fly out to Ibiza on a cheap flight and get another week's holiday on the proceeds. It had to be the last hour of the last day, because as soon as people tried them and found out they were no good, that they weren't ecstasy, they'd be looking for us. Mallorca is only a small island, and it's not difficult to find someone.

We spent a few nights in the nightclubs sowing the seeds,

saying to people we were going to get them on this particular day, and we even bought some real ones and let a few people try them, to get the word out about how brilliant they were. We bought cheap flights out to Ibiza, for the same day as Stella and Sam and them were flying home. Then on the last day, an hour before we had to be at the airport, we blitzed Magaluf and we sold them all, to the English boys that worked outside the nightclubs.

It all turned a bit sour with Stella at the end though.

Tenko was a lot younger than Stella, and on the last night of the holiday he was down in the bar and Stella was upstairs in her room, and Sam and me got really drunk and were having a bit of a go. We were saying, 'What do you see in Stella then?' And: 'You know she's got loads of blokes, don't ya?' We told him a lot of things about her. We didn't mean it, we were only having a laugh, being bitchy like women can be. But Tenko went straight back upstairs and grassed us up and it caused an almighty row. Really bad row – she stopped talking to us.

It wasn't so bad for me because I wasn't travelling home with her – I was selling the earache tablets then going on to Ibiza with Steve. But Sam had to travel home with her.

I rang Sam as soon as I got home. 'Thanks a fucking lot for that,' she said, and launched into an impression of Stella trying not to speak to her on the plane all the way back to England. There was never any question, we were going to become friends. And I've got Stella to thank for that friendship I suppose – one for inviting me out there and two for buggering off with Tenko and leaving me and Sam to it.

Sam was a loyal friend to me for twenty years. We had some mad times together – not just in Magaluf but over all them years. We were made of the same kind of stuff, we understood each other, and there was nothing I could ever say or do that would faze her. We would spend hours on the phone just taking the piss out of people – usually Stella – and making each other laugh. She had this giggle and once she started I used to start. She was my mucker, my mate. She was always there for me, through all my ups and downs, and I was always there for her. Out of anyone, I would say she became my best friend.

But for all that, she was straight, a proper person, not into anything dodgy. Sam and her husband Phil ran a demolition firm. And I remember sitting down with her on the beach one day on that holiday in Magaluf, and she gave me a talking to. 'Your life,' she said, 'what you're doing, it's no way to go on.' She knew Chopper's Charlie and how he lived his life, and how he treated women. 'I don't know what you see in him,' she said. And there's no doubt about it, he was ugly. If you saw him on the street, you would not put him on the top ten beautiful men list. 'You could do so much better, because you're not stupid,' she said. She couldn't get her head round why I put up with it. And then, 'Why don't you settle down a bit, straighten out a bit, get yourself a proper job. You'd be a lot better off.' All that.

It made sense to me. She seemed to me like someone who knew what she was talking about. She was four years older than me, and a businesswoman running her own company. And I decided that's what I was going to do.

8

GIRL ABOUT TOWN

Oh, those were my glory years! In no time, I had it made – I had it all going on.

I really took Sam's talk to heart, and when I got back from my wild week in Ibiza with Steve I started looking in the newspapers for a proper job. It was July, just before the new registration cars came out on 1 August, and there was an advert in the *Romford Recorder* for a temporary job delivering new cars for Eagle Ford, the Ford dealership in Ilford. It didn't need any qualifications and the pay wasn't bad. So I went for the interview, with quite a young bloke, he must have been in his early thirties, and he gave me the job. It was just driving cars around. Picking them up from compounds and driving them over to the dealership. Or driving them to the body shop if customers had asked for extras like colour-coded bumpers. Running errands. I didn't mind it because the day flew. It was the first real job I had ever had in a proper company. I quite enjoyed it.

And then, in my third week of being there, the girl Trudie on reception went off sick for a week and they had no one to cover for her, and they threw me on there. And I quite enjoyed that too. And because I coped so well with answering the phones and all that, the service manager – who I knew anyway from school, Paul Stephenson – he went to the director and persuaded him they should offer me something permanent. 'Listen,' he said, 'I think there's potential in this girl, she's not stupid. Why don't you offer her the chance to do something constructive?' He had been around a bit himself and he loved me to bits. Next thing I know, the service manager comes to me. 'Would you consider being a warranty administrator for us, if we put you on a motor company course? There's one next week, would you go on it?'

'Yeah,' I said, 'I wouldn't mind.' So they sent me off to Daventry and I got to stay in a hotel there, all paid for by the Ford dealership, and learned how to be a Ford motor company warranty administrator. Then they sent me on another course, to learn how to use their computer system, and I got to know how the whole company worked. I came back and they gave me a uniform and my own office and I went to the pub with my work colleagues and felt like part of a team. I'd found a job I enjoyed, I was good at it, learning more each day, and I was making good money. I was so impressed with myself. I started thinking, I'm going to sort my life out, once and for all, I'm going to get myself sorted. Course this was something I should have been doing at seventeen, not starting at twenty-four, but better late than never.

I decided to buy myself a car, my first car. Someone I knew working in the Ford system had a Ford ticket that could get me 30 per cent off, and for the first time ever I could get finance for the rest of it, because I had a proper steady income. My mum had let me move back in with her now as well – Chopper's Charlie wouldn't be looking for me anymore because he had a new girlfriend in situ – so I didn't really have any other major outgoings. I loved that little car. Brand-new Fiesta XR2i.

After a couple of years of living with my mum, or with boyfriends on and off, I decided it was time to get myself my own little flat, my own place. They'd been training me up to do more and more things at Ford and my money was going up with it. I looked in the paper and found four brand-new flats just being built in Collier Row, where I had lived as a child before we moved to the council house in Harold Wood, and I went round to have a look. They weren't even finished, it was still a building site, and the bloke there said I was the first one to look at them and I could have my pick. I could have the spec different if I wanted too.

It was a mistake even going there. Because I walked in there and once I'd seen these flats I had to have one. I wanted the one on the ground floor. It was going to be my own little place, my first place, something for me. I wasn't going to be able to settle for anything less now I'd seen it. It was beyond my reach, really, much dearer than I could afford, but that's how it is with me. I always want what's beyond my reach. The building society give me a mortgage for most of it, based on my wages, and I was going to have to find my own way of getting the rest.

Once I had the flat, I had to furnish it all nice too. And, again, it was champagne tastes and beer man's money. Everything had to be just so. Everything had to match. I wouldn't have second best. I didn't believe in buying cheap and upgrading later – I couldn't settle for it, I wanted what I wanted now.

I had the ceiling Artexed in a fancy design, all fancy flowers, really over the top. Proper light fittings, like pink chandeliers in the bedroom. The walls painted pastel greens and pinks. Widescreen TV out of Comet, which was all you could see in the little front room. And I remember sitting at some traffic lights on the way to work one morning and looking in the window of a shop called Valfields that used to sell really expensive furniture, really well-made stuff, like you would get in John Lewis. It had a three-piece suite in the window – white with all patterns on it, pink and green peacock and flower patterns – and it had big cushions like beanbags, really lovely, and I couldn't take my eyes off it. The lights must have gone green and red again and I couldn't move. I went to work but all I could think about was this three-piece suite. I went back down there in my lunch break and sat on it and it was £3000. This would have been 1989, maybe 1990, and my whole year's salary was £13000. But I wanted it. I had to have it. So I said yes there and then. And matching curtains too, made from the same material, that they had sent from the factory, that I then had to get a curtain-maker to make up, with all the swags and tails and reinforced pelmets because the material was so heavy. And macramé-lace curtains for my bedroom, £120 a window. There was a six week wait for it all so I had that time to get the money together. I stopped going out for a bit – that's how much I wanted the right suite and the right curtains. Saved all my wages. But that wasn't going to be enough.

I was so happy when I got it all how I wanted. It was my pride and joy that I had worked hard for and no one was going to take it away from me. I looked forward to going home there at night and shutting the door.

And then it was time to upgrade my car and I got the brand-new XR3i Cabriolet, top of the range. Beautiful.

Don't get me wrong, I was still out on the rampage all this time, I was still pally with Stella and Sam, doing what I shouldn't. I'd taken it down a notch because I was getting my teeth into this job now. Weekdays I was sensible. But the weekends I was still out and about. I was a girl about town and I had it all going on.

A night out with Stella was never dull. Never. I've never met a woman like it. You'd go out on a Friday and you never made plans for a Sunday because you knew it wasn't happening. You'd lose the whole weekend.

Cocaine had come onto the streets now and I got introduced to that. It was much better than the whizz, because you got the high, and you'd still drink for England, but you didn't get the comedown. So you could take it and then when it wore off it was all right, you could function. Plus, whereas speed killed your sex drive and gave men little willies, cocaine was an aphrodisiac. No one wanted the speed now, it was the cocaine they wanted – 'Get me some Colombian marching powder.' But because of that it was much more expensive. Around £60, £70 a gram when it first came out whereas whizz was £15 a gram. The rich man's drug. And the Es were out by now and they were a big thing too. I reckon I was one of the first people to have one round here, 1986. About five of us all took them together down the local pub and we all came up at the same time, it was brilliant. Never smoked cannabis though, that wasn't for me. I liked to say, I lived in the fast lane, not the slow lane.

We still went to the pubs and clubs, but we were raving now too. We used to go to riverboat raves up in St Katharine Docks. Not so much the raves in the fields, I wasn't a field person back then. (The boats didn't go anywhere, they were moored at the docks.) Me and my brother both used to go, and Stella, and one night my mum came too. It was a proper rave, the music was mental, and we were all getting it on, all hitting, with speed and Es. There used to be lovely ones in those days before they started putting all the rubbish in them. It was a marketing thing – they put out really good ones with double the amount of MDMA in them at first, and then once people were hooked they cut the dose down so you'd have to buy more to get the same effect. A lot of what gets sold now hasn't got any MDMA in at all. Back then though, they were proper. They all had nicknames – Double Dubs and Flying Saucers – and different ones did different things to you. Some made your heart beat really fast, some made you feel like you were on a roller-coaster, some, when you first come up, you could be sick, but then once you'd been sick you were happy from then onwards – it was full steam ahead. The ones that made you sick you usually found there was some smack in them somewhere along the line. They all made you feel really happy and like you loved everyone and wanted to cuddle everyone. It was the best feeling ever.

And my mum was dancing like everyone else, just copying their mental rave dance moves. Everyone was saying to me, 'You're well out of order, giving your mum an E.'

And I was saying, 'She ain't had one.'

'No, look at her,' they said. They couldn't believe she was dancing like that if she wasn't on drugs. But she's got this mad dance anyway, like a puppet dance, where she moves her arms around all jerky, so this was quite good for her, quite easy, and she was really going for it.

My mum likes to say, 'I've never had a drug in my life, never in my life. Never, never, ever, ever, ever, ever. Never.' But she has. One time me and Gary made her take poppers, just to make us laugh. You smell them and it only lasts for about a minute, but for that minute you can't stop laughing. You get a massive head rush and your face is blood red and everything is really funny. And then it wears off. You can do it about four times before it gives you a really bad headache. They sell it in sex shops, call it Gold and Rush. Anyway it was really cheap, three for a tenner or something, so we all used to do it for entertainment, take it in turns, sitting in the front room. This particular time, she was upstairs in bed and me and Gary had some mates round and we went up to her and went, 'Smell that!'

She said, 'I can't smell anything,' and laid back down and then the rush came and she went 'Ooooooooohhhhh, oooohhhhhhh' clutching her head. Me and Gary thought it was so funny.

Stella was still the same, she'd still do anything to cause a scene. I used to love the way heads would turn as we walked in, and the way you knew that sooner or later the biggest group of blokes in the bar would come over. And she couldn't ever be bored, so if it was quiet, even for a moment, she'd have to do something about that. She'd go into the toilets in a pub and come out wearing a bin bag just to make a big entrance. If she couldn't make it happen somewhere, we'd move on. Like a naughty child really, she had the devil in her all the time.

Mostly we'd leave on our own. Blokes were a nuisance, they got in the way of us having a laugh. Some nights though we'd pick up blokes and take them back to Stella's house and the party would carry on there. We'd drink more, take more gear, and then get back out again, up to no good. Stella's taste ran to younger men. She liked a nice toy boy. She'd take them back at the end of the weekend, and Sam and me, we used to joke about it, say she'd taken them captive. Because we reckoned when these geezers woke up, and saw her wig on the bed, and her all without her make-up on, they must have thought, 'Fucking hell, what's that?'

'He's still round me house!' Stella would announce on a Tuesday morning, when she had gone off to work. And Sam and me we'd wet ourselves laughing, and say to each other, 'Stella's kidnapped another one.' She did that to John Bindon once, took him home and kidnapped him for three days because she'd heard he had a big cock.

She took me to Holland with her once, on a business trip. The company paid for it. And somehow she ended up taking two young boys with her that she knew from Romford

Market. And somehow on the way home, one of them stripped and ran around the top deck of the ferry naked. That's how it was with Stella. Things happened.

We started going on beanos together too, beanos to Margate. They were a big thing years ago and Sam introduced me to them when I was just back from Ibiza. If you haven't ever been on one, you wouldn't believe what goes on. You've never seen anything like it. The best way I can describe it is it was an all-day drinking binge and shagathon. And these beanos to Margate, most people did just one a year, but they ran all through the summer, every week.

The first one I went on, I couldn't believe it myself. We all met up at Gallow's Corner and got on the coach, fifty-two of us, all women from Ford Motor Company plus Sam and Stella. Most of them respectable married women. And it was like they'd been let loose for the day. We started drinking on the coach. And speeding – someone had got speed for us all. And as we passed other coaches, full of men going down to Margate, the women would all put their faces up against the windows and wave and shout and scream. And the men on their coaches would put their arses up against the windows. And then some of the women would get their arses out too and their tits.

We stopped off for about half an hour at the Roman Galley, a great big brick Whitbread pub on the main road just outside Margate. That's where all the beanos stopped off on the way into Margate, and where they all came back for the evening too – and where the coach exploded when they went on 'The Jolly Boys' Outing' on *Only Fools and Horses*. So there were twenty-five coachloads of people all congregated there, checking each other out, earmarking anyone decent, trying to find the arses they'd passed on the motorway earlier, and working out who they were going to make a beeline for when they came back there later in the evening.

We got to Margate about eleven o'clock in the morning and parked up with all the other coaches.

All along the front there were loads of pubs, and there was a nightclub that was open from midday. We went in there, and it was like it was night-time. And with me and Stella, you could see them thinking, Oh God, here we go, as we walked in. Danced and drank and speeded for about six hours. The club had those little high round tables where you could go and stand with your drinks and Sam gave me a leg-up onto one of them and I was dancing up there, going mad. The blokes were all watching and egging me on, even though I didn't need any encouragement really, and the bouncers tried to get me down but I wasn't having none of it. They had to carry me off there in the end.

Then Stella took us to this old-time place that had a pub on the ground floor, a piano-hall on the first floor, with old people singing songs, and a nightclub open all day on the top. And we were running up and down and in and out of all the floors causing mayhem in all of them.

And then come six o'clock we all rolled out onto the streets, adjusting our eyes to it being daytime. Because all the coaches had to be out of Margate by half past six, because of all the troublemakers.

Then we all piled back on the coach and everyone got changed into their slinky numbers while it drove us back to the Roman Galley. That was where the fun really started, from then until midnight when the coaches left and took us back to Romford.

By ten o'clock at night everyone had paired off and was getting shagged outside in the car park behind the coaches, or in the fields, even on the coaches. I walked outside and I couldn't believe it, all I could see was bodies everywhere, all of them at it, all these young blokes with these married women who had husbands at home. I suppose for the women it was their one time in the year of getting drunk and losing all their inhibitions and having young blokes making advances towards them. And for the blokes, it was better than paying for it.

I never shagged behind the coaches. I didn't need to. I wasn't married, I could go out and have sex whenever I wanted. What I loved was the drinking and the speeding and the dancing and the causing uproar. Once I'd done the first one, I was smitten.

One time I remember we ran out of money and we had to bet on Stella. Because she could drink a pint so quickly, we went round betting all the men she could beat them. Fifty quid, and they all chipped in to watch the race and I knew she was going to win. We made the money, and Stella got drunk in the process.

We bet on Stella at Ascot once too. Ascot's just a toffs' beano really. We started betting with some posh blokes about what raindrop would go down the window and then we lured them into a drinking contest. I said, 'Have a race with one of them, Stel.'

And she said, 'No, you know I can't do it.' She let herself

be persuaded to try with a half, and let him win, and then she pretended to sulk for a bit. Then it was, 'Sod that, you've taken £10 from me, let's try a pint this time.' And then she slaughtered him.

I used to have my beano outfits. Skin-tight all-in-ones with a big belt round the middle, or leggings with a leotard underneath – I used to get them from dance-wear shops. And my hair all big and mental. And these trainers that I used to call my beano boots. Little black ankle-boot trainers with stars on them. I had to buy four or five pairs at a time because they never found their way home. I used to always come home from a beano wearing only one of them.

This was my summer for about five years, until I got banned from Margate for life. Sam and me both did. One night, on the way back, after we'd left the Roman Galley, the coach stopped at some services at about midnight and we all got out. I'd been asleep and really they never should have woken me up, but everyone was getting off and Sam wanted me to go with her to get something to eat. Well, we were queuing up at these services and everyone had had plenty to drink and some men from another coach party started jumping the queue. Sam and me, we weren't having that, so we started saying things, arguing with them. Sam liked to goad me a bit. She was saying, 'You don't wanna upset her, she'll knock you out,' that kind of thing. We got to the front of the queue and Sam asked how much the Black Forest gateau was. I think it was £1. 'I'll have them all,' said Sam. I knew what she was getting at. I picked up two pieces, and Sam picked up two pieces, and we launched them at these blokes. That was it – it was a free-for-all, cakes everywhere. Security came and I didn't help myself there because the security guard was so short I asked him whether he was security for Mothercare.

We went home in disgrace and I think after that the beano coaches never stopped at those services again. I remember waking up the next morning in my bed and thinking what's that smell and finding cream in my hair. Really awful. And Sam somehow managed to get herself back on the next summer, but none of the coaches would let me back on again.

A job I loved, a top of the range car, my own flat, and friends to go out with. I even got a promotion at work, to a garage in Chigwell that was closer to where I lived. I felt good about my life. Of course, with me, things couldn't be quite that simple.

First thing that made things messy was blokes. I found myself another bad boy of course. Name of Danny Tyler, out of Barking. Everyone knew him round there, he was known as a wide boy and a fighter, and for having a right hard nut. A group of us was out at the grab-a-granny in the Jake & Elwood's down in Barking one Thursday night. I had my hair all ringletty back then, permed and highlighted, and then I'd turn my head upside down to spray it with hairspray so that it would be really big. We were all laughing and joking and then I was lighting my fag and I managed to catch my hair on fire. I didn't even realise. First thing I knew of it was this bloke had run through the crowd and started patting his hands all over my head. I went, 'Fuck, get off, what are you doing?'

It was this Danny Tyler, and I thought he was really nice-looking – lopsided mouth but good-looking apart from that – and I give him my number.

Danny Tyler had a wife, Marie, and three kids, but he was away from them when we met. We were together for about eighteen months and I ended up moving in with him, into his little bedsit on the Ripple Road council estate in Barking. This was before I had my little flat.

That was a very volatile relationship though, very fiery, we were always fighting. Really serious fights. I remember one time we were rowing over at his bedsit, and he had a chandelier there that I'd given him. He turned the electric off and ripped it out of the ceiling. Well I grabbed it off him and run off with it into the street, and I remember throwing it in the road and jumping all over it, with all these people sitting on the bus watching. He used to hit me, and I'd hit him back. He used to hold me down and I'd try to bite his face. I tried to run him over once. And I was always leaving and going back to live at my mum's. And he'd deny it to me but I knew he used to go back to his wife, because me and Marie would speak on the phone.

I got pregnant by him. I would have loved to have kept the baby, but the situation wasn't right. He had three kids already and he couldn't keep a proper job down. He had a good trade – he was a scaffolder – and his brother had his own business where he used to work now and again but it was only when it suited him. I couldn't ever have relied on him bringing the money home. I went and booked an abortion and he found out and went to my dad to get him to ring me at the abortion clinic and try to stop me.

Born chirpy! Me as a baby

Still smiling. Me about three years old

Mum working on Dad's fruit & veg stall, Romford Market, 1960s

Me in the winning
netball team, top left

Me and Gary
driving Charlie

Family holidays in Spain in the mid-1970s

Me, aged 12, brother Gary, aged 10, and
Mum, winning Miss Coral Playa 1976

Barbados, early 1980s

Uncle Norman, me and Stella, in Magaluf, around 1990

Getting plastered on day release, 1994

Wedding No. 2. Second biggest mistake of my life! 1996

Prison photo at
Highpoint, 2002

Me and Mum on first
day release from East
Sutton Park, 2004

Home leave for
Xmas, 2006

Finding my forte – washing a pig in prison greens, 2006

She's out! February 2007

Me and Dad at Gary's wedding, 2008

The Giggly Pig
on the road

Two little
porkers!

Three in a bath

Down on the farm

Me and my girls!! Sausage, Mash, Gravy and Chops

Mum loved him, absolutely loved him, because he was really funny. Dad loved him too. He's a proper nutter now. His eldest boy that he always talked about got run over by an articulated lorry. That killed him, sent him mad.

Then there was the little matter of my first marriage. Bloke called Mitchell Binnington. I must have been about twenty-six when I met him, on day two of an all-weekend bender. We'd been out all Friday night, gone on to the steakhouse, left there, gone to the Early House and by this time it was about eleven o'clock on the Saturday morning and Stella wanted to go to some pub called the Coach and Wagon I think it was. 'Mitchell will be there,' she said. He was another friend of Stella's, another bad boy; his dad used to hang around with the Krays, and Stella had been with his brother Bobby before. This Mitchell was a bit of a standing joke because he'd been married so many times and had kids by so many different people, I think he's got about twelve of them. His nickname was Ding Dong Wedding Bells.

Well, I obviously found the joke quite funny, because I ended up marrying him too. And really, now, I couldn't tell you why I did it. He splashed a load of cash the first few times he took me out, champagne and that, and took me to places where everybody knew him, and that quite impressed me. And he was quite nice-looking. An angelic kind of face – pale white complexion and dark thick hair parted on the side and wavy. I think I must have been off my head when I agreed to it and then I just got swept along with it all. Stella took over. Booked the registry office, Langtons. Had a dress made. Booked a reception in the local pub. I only knew him four months and I married him – 24 May 1991.

I got really drunk at the wedding. And I woke up the next day in my bed in my flat and I looked at my wedding dress on the floor, and the presents everywhere, and I looked down and saw him in the bed, and I thought, Oh God, what have I done? I immediately regretted it. That very first day.

And it was awful the way he found out. Sam had a massive big barbecue the next afternoon at her house, and Mitchell and me went to it. I was feeling sick about the wedding, and I was standing in the kitchen with my brother Gary and all his friends. I said to Gary, 'Oh God, Gary, I have made a really grave mistake. You've got to help me get out of this.'

He made a funny kind of face at me and said, 'You're joking, ain't ya? You're joking.'

'No. I'm not. I don't know what I'm going to do.' And the toilet door opened, and Mitchell came out and he'd heard it all. It went deadly quiet in the kitchen and everyone was looking at me. Mitchell walked past me, got in my car and drove off.

I didn't go home for a couple of days. I thought it was all ruined. And then I decided I had to try to bluff it out, give it a go. So I went back and I tried to make it work. Said that, 'I didn't mean it, I was drunk.' But he knew.

We both tried to paper over the cracks for a while. But when I look back, it was never going to work. Like, what I'd thought he was, he wasn't. I'd just assumed he had loads of money. That's how naive I was. But I started to realise what he did to get it. His life was, he'd go out for three hours a day, nicking people's garden furniture out of pubs and things like that, and selling it on. Two or three hundred quid for three hours' work, and then he'd lie on the sofa the rest of the time, watching telly. This was when I was holding down a proper job. I was going to work, and he was out nicking then lying on the sofa. I'd come in at six o'clock and the bed wouldn't be made, nothing would be done. Plus he still had his flat in Wanstead and I still had mine, which wasn't like a normal marriage.

And the worst thing for me was, he used to cry. When we rowed, he'd cry. Or just if someone else in the family upset him. It was like living with Tiny Tears. To me, I'm quite a hard person and that was the biggest sign of weakness in a man, and I couldn't stand to see it. I couldn't respect him if he cried.

One day I got home from work and found him lying on my sofa. I said, 'Do you mind leaving?'

He didn't even take his eyes off the telly. 'What d'you mean?'

'Would you mind leaving?'

I got his attention now. He sat up. 'What d'you mean?'

'Well, I tried it, I don't like it, I don't want to be married anymore.'

'You're joking.'

'No, I'm not joking.'

'You haven't given it a chance.'

'I don't want to give it a chance. I made my mind up.' With me, once I decide something, that's it, there's no going back.

He went back to his flat, but the next day, and for a while after that, he kept ringing me up, asking me to go back with him, or coming round the dealership. I wasn't interested. I was back out on the rampage with Stella and Sam by now. I just obliterated him, erased him from my life, as if he had never existed. Then he gave up. Within a year of us getting married, he'd divorced me for unreasonable behaviour. The divorce papers said things like: 'Goes out on a Friday, comes home on a Monday.' And: 'When I ask to go out with her and her friends, she doesn't let me.' When I look back on it now, I don't think I ever really had feelings for him.

The second thing, after blokes, that made my life more complicated than it needed to be, was money. The money coming in from the Ford dealership wasn't enough for me and the lifestyle I wanted to live. When I couldn't find the deposit for the flat I had to have – after the mortgage I could get on my wages, I was still about fifteen grand short of what I needed – I had to find other solutions. I had five months to get it together because that was when the flat was going to be ready. I started selling weed again, and whizz, and then cocaine.

I started kiting again too. Shoplifting. I'd lift Mum's whole weekly shop from the Co-op in Harold Hill and keep the money she gave me for it. Got away with that for months before they cottoned on. Selling snide clothes, really good Armani replicas and Burberry replicas out of the boot of my car down the pubs, selling copy fireworks, buying stuff off shoplifters and selling it on. I was always good at selling, must have sold 3000 pairs of Armani jeans. Anything to make ends meet.

And then once I'd got that money together for the deposit for the flat, I needed more to kit the flat out how I wanted it. My wages were all going on the mortgage and the bills and the car finance, so my whizz money was my living money. For food and going out and doing up the flat.

I started small, just selling to people in my circle – I didn't class myself as a drug dealer. But because what I sold was such good quality I started to get a bit more known for it. You can sell cocaine any way you want. You can put lots of crap into it, or you can let it go out without much in it and that way it lasts longer and gives you a better high. I didn't ever put too much with it. I used to let it go out how I would like to take it. No one likes putting stuff up their nose when they don't know what it is. And people came back and the word spread and instead of buying one they would buy in twos and threes so I would earn my money quicker.

And there'd be times when I was the only one with my phone on. Over Christmas, or at three o'clock in the morning, people couldn't get hold of their normal dealers and they didn't want the party to end. They'd come to me, and then they'd realise my gear was always good, and that's how it went.

I still didn't class myself as a dealer though. To me that was being out on the streets dealing. I was just providing a service and earning myself a bit of pocket money. Just feeding my friends so I could feed myself. That is really how I saw it at the time.

9

THEY'RE NOT MINE

It was a normal working day for me, in February 1992. Six o'clock in the evening and already dark outside. I'd driven myself home from work, parked my new car on the driveway in front of my bedroom window – I'd just shopped in my old one for a special edition XR3i Cabriolet – and let myself into my little ground-floor flat. I was twenty-seven years old and I remember thinking to myself, This is nice. My life is pretty good.

I turned the lamp on, turned the telly on, lay down on the sofa. And that's when the knock on the door came. Actually not a knock, more of a buzz.

My flat was one of four in the block and it had its own front door inside the building, so I had a little intercom system so I could buzz people in through the main door without having to leave my flat. I was expecting a friend, a bloke called Trevor, who had his own key, so the first time the buzzer went I just carried on laying there. It went again so I got up and said into the intercom, 'Can I help you?' The first thing they said was all muffled, I couldn't hear it.

'Can you repeat that?'

'It's the police.'

'Yeah?'

'Can you open the door please?'

I hung up the intercom, and went straight out of my flat to open up the main door into the block. The police admitted that afterwards. I had no reason not to, because I knew I had nothing to hide. I didn't need to even think about it. I was dealing cocaine, but I didn't have any in my flat.

There were three of them standing at the door. Three men. I opened the door and stood in the doorway.

'Hello, are you Tracy Mackness?' said the one who seemed to be in charge.

'Yeah.'

'We're Romford CID. We've got a search warrant to search your house for drugs.'

'Drugs?' I said, very casual, not at all disturbed.

'Yeah, drugs.'

'What sort of drugs?'

'Controlled drugs. Class A.'

'I don't know what you mean.' I shrugged.

'Are you going to let us in?'

'Yeah, you'd better come in.'

The three of them followed me into my flat. 'Right,' said the one in charge, 'we're going to search the flat one room at a time.' That was fine with me. There was nothing there for them to find. 'We'll start in the bedroom, shall we?'

I was surprised they didn't want to start in the kitchen, or the bathroom. But they went into the bedroom and I followed them in. The one in charge was going through everything in my wardrobe. Not chucking everything out like they didn't know where to start, just going through the pockets of all my clothes. I wandered back out into my front room. 'Can you come back in here? We want you present in the room while we're searching.' I went back in.

Then the two others picked up the mattress off my bed and threw it into the air. And under where the mattress had been, in the middle of the bed base, just like that, was a bag. Not one bag, but twenty little see-through plastic bags, like you would use to keep buttons in, all bound together round the middle with an elastic band. And in each bag were pink tablets – it looked like ecstasy.

'Oh, what have we found here?'

I couldn't understand what was happening. My brain froze.

'What are these then, Tracy?' they said, cocky now and pleased with themselves.

'I don't know what you're on about. I've never set eyes on them before in my life.'

'Well how do you suppose they got here then?'

'I do not know.'

I kept looking calm on the outside, but I went into a panic on the inside, racking my brains, trying to think who might have left them there after we'd been out partying one night or something, because I had never seen those tablets before.

'Right,' they said. 'We're really going to start searching now.'

There was a big performance then. They got a sniffer dog

down there. Radioed through for a woman police officer when I started creating about that – because I knew there should have been one there if they were going to search a female. Turned everything in the flat upside down.

The worst moment, the moment when I had to work hard to keep breathing, was when they went through my hand-bag. I'd been hiding my gear at my friend Trevor's flat in Gidea Park. He got his rent paid for him, housing benefit, and our arrangement was because he didn't have his own bank account, the rent got paid into my bank account and I gave him the money. The counterfoil from the latest cheque, with his address on it, was in my handbag. They found the counterfoil, looked at the address, and threw it on the side. I had to force myself not to look at it. I could feel it there, as if it was beeping and glimmering. I was just waiting for them to realise what it was and pick it back up. If they'd gone to have a look at that address, they would have found my gear. But they didn't.

They were there for about an hour and in that time I man-aged to calm down. I stopped panicking, got my breathing back to normal. I started to get back to the feeling I'd had before, that this was just silly, and laughable, and I had noth-ing to hide. I was just sitting on the sofa in my front room saying over and over again that I didn't know – and it was true, I really didn't know – how those tablets came to be here. They didn't find anything else, no drugs, no money, nothing.

They took me down to Romford police station and they kept me there for three days.

In hindsight, I was in shock, and in complete denial. I didn't take anything with me – no clothes, toothbrush, anything. They asked me in the police car: was there anyone I wanted to ring, to let them know where I was? I said no.

'Do you want a solicitor then?'

'No, I don't need a solicitor.'

'Well, we do suggest you get a solicitor.'

But I didn't think I'd be there for long. They had got out of my flat without picking up that piece of paper with Trevor's address on it. There was no reason for them to go back to the flat now, I was home free on that one. And they had no grounds on the ecstasy tablets, they weren't mine. So I was feeling cocky again now, smug, elated even, like it was some big joke. I'd been in so many police stations before, I knew my rights, I knew how to play this game, and this time I hadn't even done anything wrong. As far as I was concerned, I didn't need a change of clothes, I didn't need a solicitor, and my mum never needed to know anything about it.

I thought they were bluffing, trying to wind me up. So after they interviewed me that night, I got a good night's sleep. I can sleep anywhere, it's a knack, and it really winds them up, because they like to think you're sweating in there, sitting up all stressed out.

But the next morning, when they came back on shift and wanted to interview me again, I began to think I needed to take it a bit more seriously. 'How long am I going to be here?' I asked; and they said, 'We'll just see.' At that point I asked for a solicitor. And I asked to notify someone I was there as well. I had to – had to ring Mum – because of course by that time I'd not turned up to work, and the dealership had started ringing round trying to find me and no one knew where I was. Mum had wound herself into a right tiswas.

You get ten minutes with the solicitor on your own. I told the solicitor the whole truth. 'My advice to you,' he said, 'is do not make a statement. Say "no comment" all the way through.' So I didn't make a statement, and I went 'no comment' on lots of things but not on everything – not on stuff I'd already talked about. In hindsight that came back to bite me.

I swore all the way through I'd never set eyes on those tablets.

'Right, Tracy, let's talk about the tablets.'

'I've never set eyes on them – they're not mine.'

'Where did the tablets come from, Tracy?'

'You're not listening. They are not mine. I've never seen them before.'

'How did they get there then, Tracy?'

'I do not know. They're not mine.'

That got quite repetitive and boring. Don't get me wrong, I have told plenty of lies in police interviews, and then you have to work hard to remember your story and keep it consistent. But this one particular time it wasn't hard at all because I wasn't lying, I was telling the truth.

Then they started down another track. 'They obviously got there somehow. It's all the people you have it with, isn't it, Tracy?'

I went 'no comment' on that.

And then, after the solicitor left, they said to me, 'Listen, Tracy, this is how it is. Off the record. We know that you hang around, and who you hang around with, Tracy. We've been watching other people, and you're everywhere. You're with this one, you're with that one. I tell you what we'll do for you, Tracy. You come and work for us.'

There was a lot of undercover in Romford at the time and obviously my face had been popping up too much, always with the wrong people.

'What d'you mean, work for you?'

'Well, you hang around with all the people. We know you do. What we propose is, you get out and about for us. Keep your ears open, listen out for us, tell us what you're hearing – tell us everything.'

'I don't know what you're on about,' I said.

'Oh yes, you do.'

'I do not. I do not know what you're on about.'

'All right. Have a little think about it. We can hold you for seventy-two hours without charging you.'

They put me back in the cell and I did have a think about it. I thought about how I just did not know where those tablets had come from.

But I still thought they were bluffing, that they'd put the pressure on then let me go. So I just treated it like a game. Thought it was a big game, and that I knew how to play it. I knew they had to let me have so many fag breaks; I knew they had to let me have water; I knew they could only inter-view me for so long before they had to put me back in the cell. I'd played that game my whole life.

And I knew I would never grass. I could not live with the name of being a grass in Romford. That wasn't ever an option. Even if my life depended on it.

'I'm not a grass,' I said immediately at the start of the next interview.

'Tracy, it's not about being a grass. If you knew how many people are on our books – people you know – you would be more than shocked. Some of those people's names, you wouldn't believe.'

'I don't even know anything anyway,' I said.

This went on and on. They were trying really hard.

'Come on, Tracy, this is off the record.'

'No.'

'Come on, Tracy, we know that you know what's going on in this area. One million per cent.'

I didn't care about all the other people who were grasses. It wasn't going to be me. I couldn't live with that name. Not just that, but if I'd grassed then I'd have had to worry about Mum, I'd have had to worry about my brother.

'Tracy, all you have to do is make a phone call once a month and tell us what's going on. Tracy, no one even knows you're here.'

And then it was into the good cop/bad cop routine because while the one bloke kept on about grassing, the other one started on something else. 'This is serious for you, Tracy. It's not a hundred tablets. It's twenty bags of five tablets. So we're not going to charge you with possession, we'll charge you with intent to supply. Possession, that's not even prison, but intent to supply, that's a big prison sentence you're looking at, Tracy.'

And then it was: 'We're going to make you out to be big time, Tracy. You can't live the way you do on what you earn.'

I didn't have kids they could threaten to put into care – I didn't even have pets. So it was: 'Tracy, you know if you don't do this for us, you're going to lose your job.'

'Do your best,' I said.

A job's just a job. And I thought they were bluffing.

It was true, I was hanging out with all the wrong crowd. And it was true I did know bits and pieces of what they were up to. I was seeing things, hearing things, seeing people, some of them really heavy people. Not necessarily doing things with them, but they trusted me, they spoke in front of me, they didn't treat me like some silly girl. You'd only ever hear them say it once – 'Don't worry about her, she's all right.' And then you'd be accepted into their company, you wouldn't be a worry to them. I would have been a prime person for the police to get onside.

But I also knew beyond a doubt, those tablets weren't mine.

I *was* dealing. And doing all kinds of other naughty things. Kiting, shoplifting, selling snide clothes. Obviously I was no angel. But this wasn't me – those were not my tablets, I had never seen them before. Es weren't even my thing. I used to take them sometimes when I went out, but I didn't ever get involved in selling them – that just wasn't for me.

And obviously they didn't know about the cocaine, because they never mentioned it. If they had known about that, they would have been all over me for it. They had nothing on me, they couldn't have, because they weren't mine.

I did find it quite funny thinking about all the care I'd taken not to get caught out on the cocaine, all the times they could easily have caught me with that, and here I was being questioned for three days about something I hadn't even done.

I used to keep the speed and the cocaine in my mum's house when I was living there. She knew it, and she hated it, but I could always talk her round, fob her off. With the speed, you couldn't keep it in the house because it made the place stink, but you had to keep it somewhere dry – if it got damp it was no good. I had all these different hiding places at my mum's house. The best place to keep it was in the freezer, wrapped in a brown bag. That made it stronger. That was my first hiding place. But she'd find it there and start shouting at me, 'I don't want it in the house. I don't want that stuff in the house.' One time she found it there while I was on holiday and put it in a Tupperware container and buried it in her back garden. It rained really heavily so by the time I got back and dug it up all the water had got in and it was a load of useless old mush. Probably £1000 worth of gear.

After that I used to hide it in Mum's shed for a while. I had a little red attaché case from when I was little girl, a little child's make-up case that I found amongst my old toys when I was back living with Mum. It was the ideal size to put my drug kit in, so I used to keep my little electronic scales in there, and my whizz and a bit of cocaine and things like that. She found it in the shed and made another big fuss. 'I don't want it in my house. I don't want it in my shed.' All that.

So I'd had to find somewhere else to hide it and I'd decided to hide it in her car. That nearly ended in disaster. She never drove anywhere anyway; she worked round the corner and I did her weekly shop for her. But this particular day, a friend had asked her to pick her daughter up from school. So Mum had got in her car and driven up to school and parked there on a double yellow. The police had come along and asked her to move and Mum had made a bit of a fuss about it: 'I'm just waiting for my friend's little girl.' Eventually after a bit of to-ing and fro-ing she moved the car. When she told me about it that evening, she had to make it sound dramatic. 'I got stopped by the police in my car today.' My heart stopped.

'You're joking?' I couldn't believe it. What if the police had had a dog with them and it had smelt the drugs?

And then there was Trevor's flat. My gear was sitting there now. How had I managed to get away with them not looking in Trevor's flat? At the time I thought it was funny. Afterwards I thought it was something else that just didn't add up. The police thought they had enough to frighten me so they weren't going to bother following up anything else.

On the third day of questioning, they said, 'Tracy, this is your last chance. You decide what you want to do. You've got ten minutes.'

But they didn't know about the cocaine, the Es weren't mine and I wasn't ever going to be a grass. I still thought they were bluffing. And I thought any court would find out the truth.

I said no. 'No. I'm not a grass. You do what you gotta do.'

10

GOING DOWN

It wasn't a bluff. Or, if it ever had been, it wasn't now. They really went to town on me.

But because in my mind all I knew was that I hadn't done it I don't think I ever really understood how serious it was for me. They charged me, they bailed me, and I walked out. Went back to work the next day, back to my normal life. I knew it would be a few months until the trial came up. At that point it was a game to me, and I thought I was going to win it.

When they get you for drugs, they immediately go to your home and go through everything. They call it the paper trail. All your bills, and how you live and all that. What you got coming in and what you got going out. So they went to my flat and went through it all – the deposit for my flat, my mortgage, my car, my phone bills, my holidays – and they pieced it together that I was living beyond my means.

After they'd gone through all the paperwork at my flat, they set to work at the Ford dealership. Opened up another can of worms there. I was on the hire department at that time, working on a new scheme called FRACs – Ford Rent-A-Car. The dealership bought cars from Ford Motor Company, got £3000 for registering them as part of the scheme, then made £120 a week for every car that they rented out. After three months they'd sell them off as demonstration cars too, so they were getting their money coming all ways. Well, I was doing something I shouldn't have been, but I was working that scheme to everyone's advantage. I knew lots of people that wanted cars – most of them were up to no good, shoplifting, or drug-dealing – and I was hiring out these cars to them whether they had the right documentation or not. Some of them didn't have driving licences, and I was just making up the details to write on the forms. We started off the scheme renting out three cars; within two months it was six and I had every car out every week, and before we knew it we were up to fifteen. My friends were getting their brand-new Fiestas; I was top seller; and the dealership was getting its £3000 bonus for every new car registered, plus the £120 per car per week, plus the money from selling them on. It was win-win. Everyone was very happy.

But the police came to the dealership with a search warrant and searched my office and the whole premises. Made themselves busy, scrutinising everything. The owners had to shut the dealership down for the day, which cost them money. And the police brought someone down there who knew about this kind of thing, and he worked out that none of the driving licence numbers were real. He worked out exactly what was going on and made a big song and dance about it. Called it 'misaccounting'.

The family that ran the dealership, a father and son, they didn't really see me for what I was. They liked me, and what they saw was that I was good at my job. When I'd first been charged, they hadn't believed that the drugs had been any-thing to do with me, and even when the police came in with their search warrant and searched the premises they didn't believe I'd done anything wrong. When the police told them about the FRACs scam, they still didn't want to sack me, they tried to keep me on. But the police put them under a lot of pressure.

Martin, the son, called me into his office. 'I'm going to have to let you go,' he said. 'I'm gutted, I don't want to do it. I don't believe those drugs were yours, I believe you on that. And OK, we understand what you've done with Ford Rent-A-Car. It wasn't right, and it could have cost us our dealership. But we still would have kept you on if we could. But they're going to keep coming back here, and they're going to make my life a misery if we don't let you go. I've got no option.' He did it as well as he could for me, made me redundant so my mortgage protection insurance would pay out to cover my mortgage for a year. They were real people.

But there I was, suddenly, without my job. The police had lost me my job, like they said they would.

I still thought I would get off though. I was adamant I was going to get away with it, because those tablets weren't mine.

*

My next move was not a clever one, I will admit it. I didn't bother getting another job because I thought the police would probably just hound me out of it. But I needed money. And a friend of mine called Aiden had put his hands on a load of counterfeit £20 notes. Really good ones, and we paid £2 each for them.

I was on bail so I wasn't allowed to leave the country. But I went and got a yearly passport in Sam's name – I used my picture and her birth certificate. And off we went – me and Aiden with thousands of pounds' worth of these twenties. We got a cheap flight to Gran Canaria in the Canary Islands and spent a week making money. We were just going into little shops, buying something stupid like an ice cream, paying with a counterfeit twenty, and taking the change in pesetas. This was before the euro. So out of every twenty we were getting £19 back and we'd only paid £2 for them. We were making a nice little fortune and had a slap-up holiday too.

I'd been back a day when the police rang me up.

'Can you come and see us. We've heard a rumour you've been out of the country.'

'No, I haven't.'

'Are you sure?'

'Yeah. No, I haven't.'

To this day, I don't know who told them. There were only two people who even knew. I went down to Romford police station and I was as brown as a berry. At this point, they didn't have proof. They'd been searching all the airlines but they didn't know to look in Sam's name, so they'd been getting nowhere. They'd been to my flat and I hadn't been there, but that wasn't proof. When they saw how brown I was though, they took me into custody and got another search warrant for my flat. And we'd actually done something really silly. The police found my holiday snaps and there was one of me, sitting on the beach with Aiden, reading the *Sun* newspaper. Well, I might as well have written the date on the photos, all they had to do was read the headlines.

That was it then. As far as they were concerned they could have me for jumping bail. It was a Saturday morning and they took me straight in front of the judge in chambers. It was hot and I was wearing my holiday clothes – a bright pink shorts and vest top all-in-one. My argument was, OK, I left the country, but I came back. Their argument was, she's done it once, who's to say she won't do it again and this time she might not come back. The judge remanded me there and then. One moment I'd been living it up in Gran Canaria. The next, I was in a minicab on the way to Holloway Prison.

Going into Holloway was horrendous. Horrendous. For me, the most frightening thing was the unknown. I didn't know anyone in there, and I didn't know what it was going to be like and I didn't know the system. I'd heard stories about women's prisons, like everyone has – bullying, intimidation, lesbians with square broom handles – and I didn't know what was true and what wasn't.

The other thing that was stressing me out was, I had nothing with me, because I'd gone straight from the judge's chambers to the prison. No clothes except the clothes I was wearing, no spare knickers, no nightie, no toothbrush. Just a phone card with one pound on it. And no opportunity for a visit until Monday.

I remember the smell – all prisons smell like this, and nowhere else does. It was a mix of cleaning products and BO from people who don't wash.

I remember walking down the landing towards the phone on the wall, in my pink all-in-one, past lots of scary people all silently watching me, and not really knowing how to work it. When I did work out where to push the card in, it was quite a tearful conversation with my mum. She was in a worse state than me so I was trying to be strong, and telling her everything would be all right. Plus I knew I couldn't cry in front of everyone else. She said she'd be there on Monday.

That first night, I thought I'd landed up in an asylum. The things I seen. People you wouldn't even think existed. Because you have to go in the hospital wing the first night, for your own safety, so they can assess whether you are going to try to harm yourself or try to take your own life. And that's where all the junkies are, screaming all night because they're coming off heroin. There's nothing you can do to help them. And all the fraggles who are so mental they shouldn't even be in prison in the first place. And the girls who think it's going to be easier doing their time if they're dosed up to the eyeballs on sleepers. Lots of shoplifters and prostitutes.

The next day they decided I wasn't going to commit suicide, and I didn't need to be on drugs, and they moved me on to the remand landing. Luckily for me, the screws knew it was my first time, and they put me in a dorm with some professional kiters, four older women who took me under their wing and showed me the ropes a bit. Things like what to do when you go down to the dining hall for the first time. Because I just didn't know. Everyone else knew what they were doing, and I didn't know. I got my round plastic tray with three compartments in it, one for veg, one for meat, one for dessert, but I didn't know what each section was for, and I didn't know what the system was, whether I should ask for what I wanted or just take it. Or what I should say to all the people asking me what I was in for. Because when you arrive on a Saturday morning, usually that means you've done something very bad like murder, and because I was so tanned they all thought I was a big drug importer. With the older women telling me what to do, watching my back, I felt safer.

It was five of us in one cell. And the toilet was inside the cell, behind a little cubicle door. We all had to use it. So we all knew if someone went in there, and if someone had a number two the smell filled up the whole cell.

I got another nasty shock when they all started strip-washing in front of me, stark bollock naked and giving it all that with a flannel between their legs. And I realised I was going to have to do that if I wanted a wash, with only the prison-issue flannel to protect my modesty.

Mum turned up on the Monday with some clothes for me. No toiletries, they had to be bought out of the canteen. No make-up. No jewellery, except you were allowed a wedding ring, small stud earrings, a watch and a cross or star or whatever on a chain. And she brought me a comb, a little white comb that I kept with me for the next twenty years. That comb's done a lot of bird. It was quite an emotional visit – the first ones are always hard.

After a few days, once they'd got the measure of me, a prison officer approached me and asked me how would I like to become a wing cleaner. Wing cleaner is a really good job in a prison. You clean all the landings, and work on the servery serving up the meals. It's a job for trusted prisoners and you get all sorts of perks.

Like, there were five of us on our own little landing, with our own single rooms, and the screws used to buy us maybe £10 worth of stuff a week – bars of chocolate, yoghurts, that kind of thing. (In return, we would do a few more cleaning jobs than we should have, or we'd dish up supper rather than them have to do it.) And we were out of our cell from eight o'clock in the morning until eight o'clock at night. A lot of the others in Holloway, they were up for twenty-two, twenty-three hours of bang-up, and everyone else was back in their cell by six o'clock at the latest. We were allowed to use the swimming pool. And there was a little telly room the five of us could use in the evenings. I remember we would watch *Coronation Street* and as soon as it finished we would get banged up. This was in the days before there were tellies in all the cells. And we could use the phone during the day. That was a big deal because it was really frightening trying to use the phone in Holloway. You'd get on the phone and there would be a big queue behind you and the whole time people would be shifting about, impatient for you to finish. Big Yardies looking at you, kissing their teeth, swearing under their breath. My whole ten minutes I would be hardly concentrating on the call, just thinking, 'Fucking hell, get me out of here.' I really was petrified. Wing cleaners even got to pick and choose what we ate: because we were serving the food, we got to pick all the best bits out for ourselves. We didn't have to have what the rest had.

So yes Holloway was an eye-opener for me. Cockroaches on the floor, six girls to a room, shooting up heroin and spewing all through the night, girls getting raped with broom handles. That wasn't just a story, that had actually just happened when I got there. Five girls had heard another girl had pushed drugs up inside her on a visit, and they had brutally raped her with a broom. And in Holloway, everyone goes on walkabout at the same time; they call it free flow, and you've got all sorts in there so that is really scary.

But once I was a wing cleaner, I found life in Holloway quite comfortable. I actually learnt a lot in those four months that came in handy later on. Like how to not show it when you're scared. Really important in prison. How to make other people a bit scared of you, even though you're frightened inside yourself. I made myself quite stand-offish, quite unapproachable, answered people's questions with one word answers, so people didn't know what to make of me. Never rude, I just used to cut it short. How not to become the person all the others harass and bully and tax and rob. How to make the system work for you.

I was on remand for three hot summer months. I remember sitting on the window ledge of my cell all day with my legs hanging out the window, through the bars, trying to get cool. And then in August my solicitor got me bailed, on strict conditions. I had to sign on every night of the week at Romford police station between five and six, and I wasn't allowed out of my flat between ten o'clock at night and six o'clock in the morning. Obviously I didn't want to take any notice of that, but the landlady at the pub knew the score, she was married to a gangster herself, and she used to say 'Why are you still here?', call me a taxi, and make me go home. It was a lot of aggravation having to live with those conditions, and I was quite happy being a wing cleaner by that point. I seriously thought about asking them to let me back in. Definitely would have done if I'd thought I was going down.

But I still thought I was getting off. That was still how I was looking at it.

My barrister thought so too. The trial was scheduled for September 1992, at Snaresbrook Crown Court, which is a massive court in north-east London. It went on for four or five days. We laid out to the jury all the things that we thought proved I didn't do it.

I pointed out – and the police admitted this, because another group of them had been watching me through my patio windows in case I done a runner – that when the police had come to the door, I had gone straight to open it. I said, 'You told me who you were on the intercom, but did I make any attempt to go and hide anything? No, I didn't.' The police admitted that too. 'Surely,' I said, 'if I knew they were there, if I knew there were drugs under the mattress, and you give me the chance to, I would have flushed them down the toilet before I let you in.' If I had known they were there, I would definitely have tried to get rid of them. But I hadn't. That's because I didn't know they were there.

And my barrister told the court they never found my fingerprints on the drugs.

The owners of the dealership put in really good reports for me, and my boss Paul Stephenson, who'd given me my first job, came to court and stood up as a witness for me, a character reference. He said what a good worker I was, how he couldn't believe it could be true. I couldn't have written it better myself. Mum was a character witness for me too.

But the prosecution made up such a case against me. They made out I was a hard-living drug-taking drug dealer, leading a life of luxury. They asked, how could I have this flat, how could I have this luxury sports car, this brand-new £22,000 Escort Cabriolet convertible, on the wages I was earning? They showed the jury tickets from a holiday to Barbados that were two years old and asked how could I afford exotic beach holidays. Oh, and by the way, she's got a number plate that says 'party animal'.

I must be guilty, because I had £700 a month coming in, and £1,500 going out. 'What we put to you, members of the jury, what we suggest to you . . .' and all that. They couldn't prove it, but they seeded the doubt. They painted a picture.

It was true, they were right, I was living beyond my means – there was a shortfall. But the shortfall wasn't as big as they made out – the car was up to the gills on HP, and it wasn't like I had children to support. And no way was I living a life of luxury in my one-bedroom flat, and a friend of mine had paid for the week in Barbados – I'd just bought the flight. As for the number plate – yes, it did say that. One of the auto-electrician boys who used to come in the dealership to fit stereos into the cars, he'd really fancied me, he fell in love with me. I wasn't interested – he wasn't my type, too goody goody – but I played along and he used to buy me flowers and that. When I'd got my new Cabriolet, he'd said he'd get me a number plate made up for it, airbrushed, and asked me what I wanted on it. So the number was done in all airbrushed letters – completely legal – and then, underneath, it said 'party animal'. Harmless bit of fun, but it worked against me big time in court.

Plus, that shortfall, anyway, could have been financed another way, not through drugs. For all they knew, I could have been a prostitute. I wasn't one. But I could have gone in there and said I sell my arse and that's how I made the money. I couldn't do that though, I'd never live it down. I'd rather go to prison than have people read that in the papers. I'd rather be a drug dealer than a prostitute.

I did try to say that I made the money from selling knocked-off goods. Because when they'd searched my flat, they'd found the Armani jeans and confiscated them. Didn't wash. They didn't believe I could be making that much from it.

The prosecution made a big deal too out of the fact I'd not made a statement, and gone 'no comment' on some of the police questions. Implied it meant something that it didn't.

'You only answered what it suited you to answer, didn't you, Miss Mackness? You gave yourself plenty of time to conjure up a story, didn't you, Miss Mackness?'

'I haven't conjured up anything, I'm telling the truth – those tablets were not mine.'

They said that when they'd searched my car, they'd found a bundle of little see-through bags, like the ones that had had the pills in, in the glove compartment. Well I disputed that. Because I'd had some bodywork done to the car the week before, and had it valeted, and I'd only had it back the day before the police knocked on my door. The bloke who had valeted the car came to court for me and told them there weren't any bags in the car when he'd cleaned it.

They said maybe there were no fingerprints because I'd been wearing gloves, and maybe I hadn't tried to get rid of them when the police came to the door because I was bluffing.

They had an answer for everything. Not a good answer, but it was enough, because they'd painted a picture by then, of me as this big-time partying drug dealer flying around Romford in her flash car. And it was my word – the word of a woman who didn't have a clean record – against the word of two police officers. They can't tell the jury about your criminal record, but that doesn't mean the jury don't know. If they don't hear 'This is a woman of impeccable character' or whatever, they can draw their own conclusions.

Mum by this point was pleading with me to go 'guilty'. 'You've already done four months on remand. If you go "guilty", you'll probably get nothing. Or get six months and do two.'

But I wasn't going 'guilty', because they wasn't mine, I hadn't done it. I still swear, to this day, and I will swear to my dying day, those ecstasy tablets had nothing to do with me. And after all I've done, and admitted to, I'd have no reason to lie about that. I thought I was going home, I thought the dealership would give me my job back. I went 'not guilty'.

The jury was only out for forty-five minutes. They came back with 'guilty'. I couldn't believe this was happening, I was absolutely gobsmacked. I'd lost my job, I'd done four months on remand, and now this. I felt I had been absolutely wronged.

It got much worse. As the judge adjourned for six weeks for pre-sentencing reports, he told me that I needed to use that time to get my house in order, because he was looking at a custodial sentence. I had six weeks to get everything sorted – rent my flat out, hide my Cabriolet away. There was no way I was letting anyone get their hands on that car.

Even then, though, I was thinking maybe a year, and I'd be out in six months.

Probation strongly advised he shouldn't send me to prison; they said it would be of no benefit whatsoever, that probation or community service would be just as beneficial.

But my record wasn't looking pretty by this time. I'd notched up three or four little things – the speed, the car, plus breaking bail. It must have looked like a pattern was beginning to emerge.

The judge gave me three years for intent to supply. I was going to prison for a long time, and I was absolutely petrified.

11

BANGED UP

It was a Friday afternoon in October 1992 when I got sentenced. I was ready to rumble this time – I had all my stuff with me in a holdall. I wasn't going to get caught out going to prison without spare knickers again. That took a lot of the stress out of it for me.

I was gutted about my sentence, gutted. Three years. I wasn't scared about Holloway though. Because now I knew what that was going to be like, I knew what to expect. I could have quite happily done all my time there, as a wing cleaner again. But I wasn't going to get that chance. Holloway was just where you got sent while they decided where to allocate you. After two weeks back in Holloway I got allocated out to another prison, to Cookham Wood in Kent, which is now a men's prison but at that time was a Category B women's and young offenders' prison. And then the fright was there all over again. It was the not knowing, the fear of the unknown.

I'd heard a lot of stories about Cookham Wood. It was supposed to be worse than Holloway. It was supposed to be full
of big Nigerians and Jamaicans, drugs mules doing fifteen-
year sentences. You don't hear so much about drug mules
these days because there are fewer and fewer coming in now
they put the dogs on the planes, but it was rife back then.
And also, it was supposed to be full of people that had done
horrible crimes – child killers, that kind of thing. I really
didn't want to go. I wanted to stay in Holloway, or go to
Rochford, which was much closer. But no, I had to go to
Cookham.

Myra Hindley was there. She was living on the hospital
wing by the time I got there, because any girl who wanted to
make a name for herself would try to attack her. She'd just
had scalding water poured over her, not for the first time, and
I don't think she ever came off healthcare after that. She was
a law unto herself, got treated like royalty. She was allowed
to swan around in her dressing gown, she had bouquets of
flowers sent in from well-wishers, fan mail – people even
sent her money. She amassed a lot of money over the years.
She was on first-name terms with all the screws – they used
to go out and buy clothes for her. People don't know the half
of it. She exercised all on her own while we were on lock-up.
And she had a woman with her day and night, Nina, who
was supposed to be helping her learn German or something
but they were up to all sorts. This Nina was allowed to just
wander round the prison – she had her own key.

About a week after I got there, a girl arrived who'd been
done for cruelty to a child. They told her in reception to make
a story up about what she'd done – they always do. But word

got round – it always does. One of the officers let something slip to someone. So then everyone was planning what they were going to do. Twenty-five of them, planning to beat her up and worse at breakfast. I'd seen this happen so many times in Holloway. A rumour started – sometimes it was true, sometimes it wasn't, but no one stopped to think about that. The girls would turn into a pack of dogs, all trying to kill this one person. Sometimes a girl would be ghosted out in the middle of the night because the whole prison was going for them. They called it ghosting because you were there in the evening, and then in the morning just gone. I didn't get involved. I never got involved in that kind of thing. I'd rather go without my breakfast. With this particular girl, by the time the officers got to her, the damage had been done.

So I was terrified all over again in Cookham. But then, like I had before in Holloway, I sussed out all the systems, and I got my little routine and I worked out how I was going to get through my time.

Cookham Wood was all single cells, with a toilet in the cell and glass in the door so the screws could look in and see you on the toilet. No privacy at all. You were banged up at eight o'clock at night and let out again at eight o'clock in the morning. No tellies in the rooms back then. And it was a working prison, so everyone had to have a job.

It all suited me quite well. For me, the way to get through my time was to keep myself to myself and keep busy. I used to have arguments with the other girls about that – from their point of view, they were already being punished just being there, they didn't see why they should work as well.

But my point of view was, if you didn't work you got bored anyway so you might as well get on with it.

I got myself a job in the garden and because I threw myself into it, looked interested, tried my best, the head gardener noticed me and put me on the strimmer. Usually you have to be working there three months before you get put on the strimmer. And then I was allowed to use the sit-down lawnmower and I was very happy, being outside all day, cracking along on the mower.

I've always liked reading, so I was right happy at night too. I'd have my little flask of water and my tea pack, with tea bags and coffee granules and whiteners and sugars in it, and my book. And bang me up at eight o'clock at night, in my own single cell, I felt safe. I wasn't going to be put in situations then, in places that I didn't want to be.

That went on for a few weeks. Then out of the blue, one day, the Governor was running through the corridor stopping people and asking, 'How long are you doing? What are you doing? What are you in for?' The prisons were all so overcrowded that they were desperate to ship people out – they needed Cookham Wood for the dangerous prisoners, or for people doing longer sentences. The Governor took me aside and asked me would I be prepared to go to another prison – an open prison, up north, called Askham Grange near York. I was a model prisoner, I worked hard, I wasn't on drugs, and I wasn't in for anything violent, so I fit the criteria. The plus side for me was, I'd be getting to an open prison much earlier than I should have been. It was much easier doing time there, you even got to go home at the weekends. The downside was, it was up north so it would be really hard for people to come and visit. Yes, you could go home, but you had to pay for your own ticket. A hundred pounds for a train fare home – most of the girls couldn't afford that. If he could get me accepted, he asked, would I go?

What the Governor didn't know was that my family all came from York. Seven of Mum's brothers and sisters still lived up there and a lot of cousins. They could take me out on the weekends. I said yes.

A few of us went up together from Cookham, which was good for me. Made me feel less anxious about the change and the new regime. But on the first home visit, two of the girls bunked the trains instead of buying tickets and got caught. So they were straight back to closed prison. Another one went on a home visit and didn't come back at all, she went on the run. And two others were doing such short sentences they were released almost immediately. So within two months it was only three of us left. Not for the faint-hearted, being the only southerners in a northern jail. They'd try to goad us into fighting, screaming at us: 'Let's go, cockney slags!' But it didn't matter by that time, it didn't bother me; I knew what I was doing by then.

I got myself a job in the kitchens. And I worked my way up until I was number one there, under the chef. I didn't really have to do anything once I had that job, just show the others what to do and watch what they were doing. Sorted. Got home for the whole of Christmas too. And got myself a room on the top floor, what we called the penthouse. The ground floor was for the youngsters, eighteen- to twenty-two-year-olds, little monsters. The first floor was for everyone else. And then the top floor was for lifers and people doing long sentences, anything over eighteen months. Three or four to a room, or singles.

The big downside at Askham Grange was all the lesbian activity. It goes on everywhere, in every women's prison. But it was horrendous in Askham Grange; I'd say about 80 per cent of them were up to it.

They used to all be snogging their girlfriends on visits. It caused a lot of fights too – either fighting between silly girls over 'bloke' lesbians, or fighting between the lesbians going at it in the dorm and the ones who didn't want to listen to all the slurping all night. One time a girl who was a bouncer caused a big fight that the officers had to sort out. She'd had enough of listening to the eating noises, and she turned the light on and started throwing boots and shoes at them.

Some of these girls, they looked just like men. They actually thought they were men. The only thing they didn't have was a cock. They would all have short blonde spiky hair, they'd walk like a man, they'd wear Calvin Klein pants and vests, and they didn't want to wear bras. And tight stuff so you couldn't tell they had tits.

The one fight I was ever in, when I was in prison, was when a huge bloke lesbian from Hull tried to cut me with a knife because I scorned her advances. I admit, I had talked to her, because she tried to befriend me and I felt a bit sorry for her, but she took that the wrong way and thought it was a sign I wanted things to go further. I'll never forget, I was in the bathroom and she tried to get in the bathroom door. I said, 'What do you want?' and she said, 'I want to come in.' I said, 'No chance – what do you want to come in here for?'

That made it worse. She started putting notes for me under my pillow. 'I really fancy you', that kind of thing. Then one day in the kitchen it all came to a head and she pulled a knife on me and was going to stab me with it. She got ghosted out the same night.

The other big downside was the bloody bell. About five times a week the bell would go off in the middle of the night. Either because someone had set off the fire alarm, or because they'd done a check and someone was missing. They'd walk around ringing this big bell – 'Everybody up!' – and whatever time it was, even if it was four o'clock in the morning, everybody had to get out of bed and go downstairs and sit in the dining room and be counted. So then we're all sitting in the dining room in our nighties waiting for the fire brigade to come, with our names being called out like little kids.

But that aside, I would say hand on heart that I loved doing my time at Askham. It was not a deterrent to me whatsoever.

There was a hostel in this prison, for twenty girls, in the same grounds but set far away from the normal prison. You had your own room, and you were allowed to go out to work. You were even allowed your own car. Really, it was all about getting you ready to go home. This was nearly twenty years ago now; it's not so easy these days. But in those days, being in a women's open prison wasn't like being in prison at all.

I sat the board for the hostel as soon as I could, in December. The officer in the kitchen was a PO, which is one of the top prison officers, one under the Governor, and even though he said I was such a good worker he didn't want me to leave the kitchen, he gave me a really good recommendation. That swung it for me, and I got my place in the hostel.

All the girls in the hostel used to work either for Rowntree's in the chocolate factory, or in the sack factory. I wasn't going to work in a sack factory or even in a chocolate factory. That was below me. The first day I was there, I asked them to let me write my CV so I could send it out to all the Ford dealerships in York. Because I had a lot of years' experience with Ford Motor Company by this point. They said OK, but if you haven't got yourself a job within a month, you'll have to go and work in the sack factory. That wasn't going to happen, so I started ringing round all the job adverts in the local papers as well. I was adamant I was going to get a job.

The same day, I asked them: could I bring my car up? I'd hidden it in Sam's barn during my trial because I didn't have the money to meet the payments, and there was no way they were taking it back. The Governor asked me what it was and I said it was an Escort. Which it was. I didn't tell him it was an XR3i Cabriolet. He let me home for the weekend to go and get it.

So that first Sunday evening on the hostel, I roared back into the prison after my weekend down south, in my bright metallic-blue sports car, a better car than most of the screws had. That didn't go down too well with the other girls for a start. And then when I got inside, there was some mail waiting for me, from a bloke called Gavin Fincham in the local Ford dealership in Tadcaster. He said he'd read my CV and could I ring him up and we'd arrange to have an interview.

First thing Monday morning, I went straight to the prison office with my letter. 'Can I ring right now?' I asked. I rang up Gavin Fincham. 'Can I come down and see you now?' I said to him. I really wanted this job.

It was quite an unusual job interview I suppose.

'What brings you to York?' asked Gavin.

'Oh, do you want the truth?' I said.

'Yes. I do.'

'I'm in prison.'

'I knew that,' said Gavin. 'I was just waiting to see what you'd say. Everyone knows what Askham Grange is around here. I was just waiting to see how you'd react. And what are you in for?'

I explained the situation. I'd been given a three-year sentence for something I hadn't done. I told him I'd been hanging around with the wrong crowd. He didn't need the whole story. So now he believes I've been really wronged.

'The only thing is,' he says. 'I asked to see you because I was so intrigued by you. And with your experience in every department, I'd be a fool not to take you on. You'd be an asset to the company. But I haven't got a job for you right now. I'll create one, but I can't do it immediately.'

'I've got a problem there,' I said. 'If I don't get a job in a month, I've either got to take their job in the sack factory, or I'll be thrown off the hostel and I'll have to go back on the prison.'

'OK, leave it with me.'

I drove back to the prison, which was about four miles away. By the time I got back there, he'd been on the phone to them, offering me a job. 'Can you send her back down,' he'd said, 'because she's got to get her uniform.' So I went down and got my two uniforms – one green and one blue. I'd been on the hostel a week and I'd got a job at the Ford dealers, and he was paying me ten grand a year. Now I was the talk of the prison and all the other girls really hated me.

And then a local pub rang me up and said I could come down for an interview for a job I'd applied for there – kitchen assistant, in the evenings. I applied to the Governor to ask if there was any prison rule that says you can't have two jobs, and he said no, if you want to do them both then you can. So I went down there – it was a family-owned olde worlde country pub in Upper Poppleton, always fully booked – and got that job too. Started off as a washer-upper and within nine months I was their grill chef, cooking up their steaks. That was Wednesday to Saturday evenings. And then I got a third job at a posh brasserie near the racecourse called The Grange, Monday and Tuesday evenings. Went for a job as a kitchen porter, ended up doing silver service waitressing for them. And they treated me not like a prisoner but just like everyone else, even split the tips with me at the end of the month.

My idea was, I don't want to be in the prison, I want to be out all day. I spent all day working at the Ford dealership, drove straight from there to the pub or the brasserie, and just went back to the hostel at eleven o'clock at night to have a shower and go to sleep in my little room. And I was allowed to keep the money I was earning. I had to put it away, I wasn't allowed to spend it, but it was mine.

It was pretty hostile, the atmosphere in the hostel – I didn't have any friends there at all, and there was a lot of jealousy because of my car and my jobs. But it didn't matter to me because I didn't intend to be there except to sleep. I didn't have time for tittle-tattle chat with anybody anyway.

When you get done for drugs, you get sentenced to your time, and then later, on top of that, you get a confiscation hearing. That hearing is for the courts to decide how much money you made out of the drugs, and how much they are going to take off you. About three weeks before I was due to get out, I got given a confiscation order for £8000. Which was quite a dirty one really, because if I hadn't been able to pay it I'd have had to do another two years on top. In the end my Uncle Norman lent me the money out of his life savings and it took me three years to pay him back. That left quite a bitter taste for me.

I'd planned to stay up in York. I had three good jobs up there. I'd told Gavin Fincham that I'd be staying on, and the people at the pub and the brasserie too. I'd even told Mum. And there was nothing for me to go back to. But the sentence hadn't changed me – it hadn't acted as a deterrent at all. And the day I got out, I just had to go home. Something was pulling me back to Romford, back to my old ways, back to trying to earn money the quickest way I possibly could. I put my stuff in my car, and drove straight home.

12

ON THE OUT

When I came out of prison I was more respected than ever in Romford – everyone knew I'd been set up by the police, and that I'd kept my mouth shut and done time for it. But at the age of thirty-one I had no money, no job, and a grudge against the system.

I was walking around with a major chip on my shoulder. Well, I'd gone into prison with a chip, now it felt more like a bag of potatoes. I felt like I needed to recoup things, get my revenge. I was really bitter. I'd lost my job, and got three years and an eight grand fine, for something I didn't do. I hadn't lost my flat, I'd managed to hang onto that, but I was back living at Mum's because I'd had to rent it out. And in my mind, no way was I getting another job. I'd done a prison sentence now – who was going to give me a job if they could give it to someone else? Fifty people apply and you're at the bottom of the list when they see where you've been.

And, of course, I'd learnt a lot in prison. And not the things I should have learnt. They say prison is the university of crime and, believe me, it is. Things you don't know when you go in there, you know by the time you come out. Whatever you might want to get up to, there's always someone there willing to teach you. Plus the people you meet, the contacts, by the time you get out, you got the network to do anything you want.

I did apply for lots of jobs and just kept getting knocked back, and then eventually I got one, at a Hyundai dealership in Hornchurch. He knew I'd been in prison but for some reason he decided to give me a chance.

And for about a year I just pottered about on my own, working at the Hyundai dealership, living with Mum, and supplementing my wages however I could.

It wasn't all illegal, some of it was just cheeky. Like the time I got Crazy Dirk, a lunatic six-foot-six Dutchman, to give me £3000 worth of Christmas trees to sell outside a garden centre. I went to the field where he was working and told him he knew my Uncle Norman, and I wanted some Christmas trees. He was wearing a big beige leather jacket with leather tassels.

'But I haven't got any money,' I said.

'What?'

'I haven't got any money.'

'What do you mean, you haven't got any money?'

'I've just got out of prison.'

'Oh really, you've just got out of prison, and you've got no money, and you want me to give you Christmas trees?'

'Yeah.'

And instead of telling me to go away, he looked at me, and told me to wait for him in his little office, in a shed on the field.'Go and sit in my office over there.'It was mad busy in his field, everyone driving up and wanting to buy Christmas trees, but he came over to talk to me in the shed. He looked intrigued.

'Why should I give you Christmas trees? What did you go to prison for?'

'Drugs.'

'Do you take drugs?'

'Sometimes.'

'There you are, snort that then.' And Crazy Dirk got out some white powder from a wrap and set out a big line of it. To prove myself to him, I took it. He took a line too. I'd been expecting cocaine but it was speed, which you don't usually snort. It was really pure too, because he was a speed freak. The two of us were like startled rabbits, frozen with our eyes wide open, and then we couldn't stop talking to each other, wah wah wah, like we had taken a truth drug, and I was off my nut for about three days. But I'd passed his test. He gave me the Christmas trees, and we became firm friends.

About a year after I came out of prison, I was out one night in the same place as this bloke Warren Walker. I already knew him from before, he used to be good friends with my old boyfriend Danny Tyler, out of Barking, and I knew he was all right, a nice bloke. Slim build, sharp features, jet-black hair and a kind nature, easy-going. He'd just done four years for cannabis, got out exactly the same time as me, so we had a lot in common. We ended up getting together that night.

But this Warren was married to Stella's daughter, Denise. Denise and Warren had got married while he'd been in prison. And even though they were split up when we got together, Denise went mad when she heard about it, and then Stella went mad too.

Really, I was more like Stella's daughter than Denise ever was. But Stella took her side. She phoned me up and was in complete uproar down the phone. 'I can't believe it, I can't believe you done this to me. Can't believe you done this to my daughter.' All of that.

I said, 'I ain't done nothing – they wasn't still together.'

'You still shouldn't have gone there.' On and on and on. We had a really bad row.

Then Stella was ringing me and Warren up all the time. 'How could you do this to me – how could you do it to my daughter?' Giving us loads of grief. And she started getting on the phone to my job every day, at the dealership, harassing them to get rid of me. 'Do you know she's been in prison – do you know what she is?' Driving them mad too.

I would have been quite happy to stand my ground, tough it out, because as far as I was concerned I hadn't done anything wrong. And now I think maybe if we'd stayed around, the whole thing would have died a death, because at the beginning I wasn't madly in love with him anyway. But Warren couldn't handle all the aggro. He decided we had to get away, make a fresh start. I packed in my job and we moved into this little run-down shack in Jaywick, near Clacton-on-Sea, and done it up.

A lot of the properties in Jaywick were more or less shacks like this one. They'd never been built to live in, they'd been built to be holiday homes, but now people were living in them all year round. This particular one belonged to a friend of Warren's who was looking to sell it. He'd said we could go down there and do it up, and buy it off him at a later date. Warren had done a lot of painting and decorating courses in prison and we spent the summer living there and working on it together, made our mark on it, made it look really nice.

And we ended up getting married, almost out of spite, I will admit, because we felt like it was just me and him really, living this dog's life that she'd driven us into. 'Come on,' Warren said, 'I'm going to marry you.' Langtons again, same as my wedding to Mitchell Binnington. Same people there more or less, except Stella. And then Sri Lanka for our honeymoon – 26 October 1996.

Me and Stella didn't speak for years after that. And Sam took my side. Sam and her husband Phil came to the wedding, even though they had been close with Denise. Phil had given Denise away when she'd married Warren, and Sam and Phil had looked after Denise's son when he was little, for about three years. So Stella didn't speak to Sam either. For a lot of years it had been the three of us and now there was this big vicious sort of thing going on.

Warren could be a lovely man and we had some good times together. But it wasn't a life. I was down there on my own in this shack in Jaywick all day. It had been fine in the summer, all the doors open, working away together on the house, but now it was winter and the wind off the sea was icy and the days were dark. Warren would drive back up to Romford to buy and sell cars or do whatever he had to do and, sometimes, if he'd had one too many drinks after work, he'd end up staying at his mum's and wouldn't come home all night. And I'd be in a shack in Jaywick on my own, all day and all night and then another cold windy empty day. No job, no friends, no money to do anything because we were both just out of prison, very isolated.

My only company was an old bloke called Dennis who lived opposite. He must have been seventy and he was a big man, overweight, used to sit eating cakes all day. He could barely walk. Used to take in young men as lodgers. And because neither of us had anything to do, I used to go round there a couple of times a week and take him out. We'd go shopping, or we'd go to the bingo. Or he'd come to me for a cup of tea, or I'd go to him. Apart from Dennis, there was a woman called Maureen who came down in the holidays with her kids and her sister-in-law. I used to look forward to that; we'd go to the bingo together, or to the club in the Martello tower for a drink. But that was my social life, that was it. And I used to think, How has it come to this? Warren still had all his friends to go out with, and I'd given up mine, and I resented it.

Sometimes Warren would come home with a bottle of vodka and a gram of cocaine, and then we'd get it on and we'd be all right for three or four days.

But then when it had all run out, he'd stop out again, and it would all go back to being awful. His partner, Perry, hated me for some reason, and I hated him. Nasty little man, bald and fat with lots to say for himself in a grating squeaky voice I couldn't stand. But Warren wouldn't have a bad word said about him, he loved him. Perry knew it wound me up when Warren didn't come home – he knew what would happen – and I used to feel as though he kept Warren out drinking on purpose.

Warren was a good-looking bloke, and a bit of a flirt. My mind started to obsess on particular things, down there on my own. My mind would run away with me – I'd imagine all sorts of things, and once the idea was in my head I couldn't get it out. I started to accuse him of going with other women, of going back with Denise, and there was absolutely nothing Warren could say to convince me he wasn't. He used to swear black and blue, but I couldn't believe him, I wouldn't be pacified. Or he'd just laugh at me, mock me. We started having terrible fights, worse and worse. He was a mellow man, Warren, very placid, he just wanted a quiet life, and as far as he was concerned he hadn't done anything wrong. He would have been quite happy just sitting and watching his old war movies on DVD, but I knew all the buttons to press and I would push him until he had to fight with me. I hit him on the head with a crystal vase once, a wedding present. He didn't hit me back, just punched a hole in the wall, in his own plastering work.

I was obsessing about having a baby as well. Warren had had a vasectomy when he was really young, when he'd been with his first wife. When we'd got married he'd gone and had it reversed. But because he'd had it for so many years, they did say there was a big chance the reversal wouldn't work. And it didn't. They checked his sperm after four months and they were dormant, there was no movement there, and they said the chances of me conceiving were very very slim. For

Warren, that was it. He wasn't prepared to do anything else, there wasn't going to be IVF or anything like that. I walked out of the hospital in tears, feeling like all my high hopes for the future had been dashed.

Finally, one night, in the middle of another screaming match, he said he was going to leave me. I wasn't the person he knew years ago, I wasn't someone he wanted to be with. He stormed out, and I took an overdose of tablets. I didn't want to kill myself but I wanted him to sit up and take notice and I couldn't think of any other way. I wanted him to try to understand what I was going through. The neighbour, Maureen, had heard the shouting through the thin walls and she came across the road and found me.

At the hospital they said I was depressed, and put me on a drug to calm me down called chlorpromazine. I knew it from prison; it's what they used to give all the prisoners years ago to keep them under control. They called it liquid cosh because of how it made you so out of it.

So I took my liquid cosh and I went back to our shack in Jaywick, in a trance.

But nothing really changed. His mum came to stay with me for a bit, and for a few weeks Warren made sure he came home every night, and that was lovely, but within a month we were back where we'd been. He was still going out and staying out. I was still on my own. I was still obsessed that he was cheating on me, couldn't think about anything else.

When I look back, it must have been a nightmare for him. And I realise now that the thing I was most worried about, him going away and leaving me, is what I drove him to do.

I wasn't myself. And this was not the life I wanted.

The illness got worse. I spent all day feeling physically sick in my stomach with the worry of it, whether he was cheating on me, always fearing the worst, reading the worst into everything. I lost all my confidence, all my assertiveness and personality, felt tired all the time, couldn't even get dressed some days. Every time he went out, I didn't want him to go. I was crying a lot.

One night when we'd both been drinking we had another massive fight and I went a bit berserk, completely lost control, ranting and raving, and I took another overdose.

I ended up in the psychiatric unit in Clacton and they said I was psychotic. Warren said, 'That's it, I've had enough,' and rang Perry to come and take him away. Warren just left me there. My mum had to come and bring me back to Romford. She tried to take me home to live with her, but I was in such a state, so out of control, having a breakdown basically. I couldn't do anything for myself, couldn't even move. Mum was bathing me, her boyfriend was carrying me everywhere. After two days she ended up calling the doctor in. They sectioned me and put me in psychiatric care at Warley Hospital in Brentwood.

I was in Warley for about six weeks. I was in bits; I lost about two stone in weight. They gave me anti-psychotic tablets to try to block out the obsessive thoughts about Warren, chlorpromazine again. The thoughts went away, but so did my mind. I was like a zombie. Warren's parents used to come and visit me, because they had always liked me. They gave Warren a hard time about it all. They thought he'd treated me badly, that he was partly to blame for making me like this and, eventually, after about a month, they persuaded him to visit. That was a bad idea because it started me off again. 'Listen,' he said, 'I'm prepared to give it one more go, me and you.' It was coming up to Christmas. 'I'll go and book us a holiday, we'll go away for Christmas.'

So I came out of the hospital and we went to Goa, for three weeks. It was all right, we didn't have any big rows. But it wasn't much of a holiday. I couldn't go in the sun because it reacted with my tablets and brought me out in a rash. Warren was letting me drink, and giving me cocaine, even though I was still on all these tablets, which was the last thing I needed. And I could see that there was something not right between us, that things weren't ever going to be the same.

We got back from holiday on the morning of New Year's Eve, 1997. We'd agreed we would try living in my flat for a bit, get me away from Jaywick. Warren took me back there and said he needed to see Perry but he'd come back early evening and get me to go out. I unpacked the cases, put a load of washing on, made some dinner. It was going to be the first time I'd been out in Romford for a long time, since before I was ill and before we moved away to Jaywick, and I was thinking about what I was going to wear, who I was going to see, where we were going to go. Six o'clock, seven o'clock, eight o'clock came and went and he didn't come home. This was New Year's Eve. I kept ringing him and he kept saying he'd be home soon. I ran a bath and lay there thinking it all over. Thinking, suddenly, that I didn't care anymore. Once upon a time I'd lain crying on the floor over this man, and now I realised he wasn't fucking worth it.

When he eventually turned up, about nine o'clock, something just clicked.

'Get ready,' he said, 'and we'll go out.'

'You know what,' I said, 'this ain't gonna work. I don't wanna go out. I'm finished with you. I'm not gonna let you do this to me anymore. You might as well go.'

'Are you sure?' he said. 'Because when I go, I'm not coming back.'

'Just go.'

And I never set eyes on him again.

13

GANGSTER'S MOLL

So now I was thirty-three years of age, living back with my mum so she could look after me, two marriages and one prison sentence behind me, in complete bits. I'd lost Stella, lost Warren, I wasn't going out, didn't have a job, no goals, I was just drifting. Sam was there for me, like she's always been there – she was my rock – and Mum, but that was all I had.

I probably drifted like that for about a year.

Then, towards the end of 1998, I started to pull myself together. I moved back into my flat in Collier Row. And I managed to find myself a job. Had to tell a few white lies to get it, because of my record; I couldn't tell them about my past.

Once you've been in prison you can't get a job. Because the law now is – you have to tell people. Before, you could skirt round it, not mention it, but now, if you don't tell people, you can go back to prison for that. So even if you haven't been to prison for thieving, no one wants to give you a job. You've got a black mark against you, a stigma. That was fine when I didn't want the job – if the Job Centre sent me for something I didn't want, I would sit down, say, 'I've got to tell you, I've been in prison,' and I could be in and out in three minutes. Played the system. But when I genuinely wanted the job, I couldn't get it.

I definitely wouldn't have been able to get this job, as a care worker for old people. I wouldn't have been allowed into people's homes. So I gave myself a different name. Used Sam's name and her National Insurance number, and had to answer to the name of Sam all day. It makes me laugh because if any of them are still alive and see me on the telly now, they must be thinking, 'I know her, but her name's not Tracy, it's Sam.'

Yes, it was wrong, but I wasn't doing anyone any harm. I never did anyone any harm. I was doing something I wanted to do, and I was doing a service. I was doing good, even if I wasn't doing it right.

I loved caring. I could go back to doing that now. I loved looking after the old people. I used to feel so sorry for them – they'd just been forgot about. And it paid really good money, much better than I could have made at a car dealership. We worked in pairs, going round to old people's houses and doing whatever needed doing. We'd get them out of bed, wash them, get their clothes on them, put them in a chair for the day. That was the early shift. Then the next shift was doing their breakfasts – 'hard-boiled egg, there you go, Stan, see you later' – and then the lunch shift, then tea, then getting them back into bed. Or for some people you would just go round to toilet them. It was £8 an hour and some days I totted up twenty hours. And I did sleepovers, where you used to have to be there in their house and if they woke up you would get up and toilet them. They were another £120 a night. I was clearing £600 a week.

I used to go above and beyond. A few times I got home but I didn't feel happy about something, and I went back in my own time, just to check everything was all right. And if they fell over when I was there, I picked them up. The care agency said you mustn't – you were supposed to wait for the ambulance to arrive – but they used to get in such a state waiting for the ambulance, so upset, that I would struggle to pick them up myself. They were so grateful.

I worked hard and I progressed quickly. Because I was single I had no ties, and I started going on call over the weekends in case there was an emergency. And a few of them started asking for me specially.

There was one woman called Doris who lived in Billericay in a little bungalow. She was a bit stuck up her own arse to be honest and she liked everything just so. All the carers hated her, no one could stick her, but for some reason she liked me. Maybe because she liked my cooking. Her daughter bought all her food from Marks & Spencer so there would be a little bit of fish and I would make something to go with it, and then dessert, and we'd sit together watching daytime television while she ate her dinner. Or maybe she liked me because I say it how it is. The first time she had a go at me I turned round and said, 'Doris, who do you think you're talking to? Don't talk to me like I'm a piece of shit on your shoe.' And she called me up after and said, 'I'm sorry if I offended you.' They took me off Doris one time after she got on my nerves too much but she got so upset I had to go back. I walked in and she said, 'Oh, I'm so pleased to see you.' And I said, 'Yeah, now you'll appreciate me, won't you?'

It definitely helped me to get over everything, having them in my life.

One day, I went round to my friend Sean's house. I'd known him since I was a kid and he had a big house round the corner from my flat. I knew that he was up to all sorts of mischief; he used to supply drugs big-time. We were just chatting, and Sean said to me, 'Do you know anyone who wants to buy any puff? I've got this cheap stuff.' And all that. Puff wasn't really my game but I remembered someone who had asked me for some before, and I made a phone call. 'Yeah,' I said to Sean, 'I do know someone, as it happens.'

The puff was in big kilo blocks and from what Sean wanted for it, and what my mate wanted to pay for it, I worked out I could make a quick two hundred quid out of each one. My mate wanted six. Sean made a call and a bloke called Frankie Farrell arrived with the blocks; he was their runner, their delivery driver. Frankie came in, shook my hand, and we got chatting. He was like a gentle giant. We had a few drinks, a line of Charlie, a laugh. I quite liked him.

Before I knew it, I was seeing this Frankie. It was February 1999 and now I had a job I really liked, and a bloke with loads of money who didn't know how to spend it.

We went out together and I kitted him out with a whole

new wardrobe. With his money, obviously. When we met it was all tracksuits and trainers but we went out and got him leather loafers and dress shorts for the summer and nice trousers. He was a different person.

Then I started to think about buying a house. A friend of mine built houses for a living, and he was building some down in Wickford. Three bedrooms, detached, high spec, just seven of them in a little cul-de-sac. I went and saw them and I really wanted one. Frankie gave me the deposit, I got the house in my name, and he moved in with me.

Frankie was a lorry driver for his proper job, he drove big lorries on the continent, but he was into drugs in a big way. He used to drive lorries full of drugs for these people, and take the lorries somewhere and empty out whatever was in there, usually shampoo, and get the drugs out, for ten grand a time. Twice a week sometimes. He was like a joey for them, but quite an important joey. This wasn't small fry anymore, this was big fry.

Which, looking back, was bad news for me because if I was seeing someone that involved, there was no way really I was going to keep myself out of it.

At first, I did stay out. I started selling puff and other bits and pieces again on the side, but I wasn't doing anything for them. I didn't have to. I had my own job, and Frankie was paying the mortgage on my house.

Frankie had a wife and kids down in Harwich he told me he had split from completely.

We used to be together for three or four weeks, and then we'd have a big row, and he'd disappear on me for a while.

He fucked off and left me for the Millennium. I was on my own for New Year's Eve again. Christmas Day I went round and got a few old people out of bed, who didn't have anyone to be with them, and then went to Mum's for dinner. I didn't understand how these old people could be on their own at Christmas when they had sons and daughters. New Year's Eve, I drank a bottle of champagne on my own, watched the fireworks on the telly, and went to bed.

Then he came back, said he'd booked a holiday for me and him in Sandals in Jamaica, that he was going to pay for everything. I'd always wanted to go to Sandals, it was a life-long dream. But before we could go, we had another row and he disappeared again. I was gutted.

I wasn't sure whether he was coming back this time, and I was worried about money. I started to take in lodgers, to cover the mortgage. One of the girls at the agency told me about a company in Basildon that did training courses, to retrain service people when they came out of the army or the navy. Trained them to be HGV lorry drivers, things like that. And this company was always looking for people to take the men in and rent rooms out to them. They gave you £80 a week each, and all you had to do was give them a breakfast in the morning and evening meal, Monday to Friday. Breakfast was cereals, just get on with it, and dinners I just used to cook a bit more than I would have done anyway and leave it on the side for them while I went out caring. And they were my entertainment. Because they all like a drink, army and navy. It was like a big game.

Then one day, out of the blue, there was a knock on the door, and Frankie was back. And all these men were in situ.

He said he was sorry about the holiday, that he hadn't been on it either – he'd cancelled it in the end – but he loved me, he wanted to be with me. I don't know why, but I agreed to go back with him.

Frankie now started introducing me to lots of bigger and better people. One time, he was going over to Holland, to talk to the people who supplied his drugs, and he took me with him.

It was a different world. They were living the high life, these people, money no object, it was mad. They'd just hop on a plane between their penthouse apartment in Holland and their villa in Spain, or they'd decide to drive it in their Merc. They'd spend a thousand pounds on a meal –'No worries, I'll get that' – there was always champagne and cocaine flowing. They all had yachts and speedboats. One place they took me to was called the Supper Club in Amsterdam. This place, you had to wait months to get in there. And when you got in, you all sat on mattresses, and transvestites climbed up ladders to serve you your dinner. It was mental.

I liked it, I wanted to be a part of it. I got quite friendly with the main man and his wife, Jo-Jo, out in Holland, and we exchanged numbers. She was about my age and a former lap dancer; he was twenty years older.

I still didn't really have anything to do with the drugs though – I was just Frankie's girl.

Frankie wasn't happy about the lodgers at first, but then he started joining in with them and getting on the piss with them and they didn't bother him anymore. He definitely didn't like me working at my caring job though. He didn't like that I had friends from the care agency that I was quite pally with who used to come round to the house. Or that I had to get up early in the mornings and he had to wait until I'd finished work for me to come home. It was quite strange for me too, living this double life. Who was I going to be today, the care worker or the gangster's moll? But I liked the job, I'd put a lot of effort and deceit into getting it, and I wasn't going to give it up and be left with no money. I'd learnt that lesson before, when I'd given up my Hyundai job and moved to Jaywick with Warren Walker.

One weekend, the people from Holland were over in England. It was the two main men, who were brothers, and their wives, and they were over for their mum and dad's 50th wedding anniversary and they had a big party in some big place up in Epping. It was a Sunday afternoon and there were loads of people there – three-course meal, champagne everywhere, matching balloons, cards – it was way over the top. Everyone was in their designer clothes – the men were casual but dressy, in Calvin Klein or Mankind jeans with gold Rolex watches. In my eyes, unless you had a gold Rolex watch you weren't a proper drug dealer. Women all in diamonds, trying to outdo each other.

And when the party ended, the main bloke from Holland said, 'Come on, let's go back to my mum and dad's place.' Frankie didn't want to go, but we went. The champagne kept flowing, cocaine, everything. Frankie wanted to leave. He kept saying, 'We're going now.' And I kept saying I didn't want to go. Eventually we left.

When we got into his car, he said, 'Next time I tell you we're going, we're going.' And he leant across and slapped me. That wasn't in his nature – he was a very mild person normally. Then he started up the car and drove off. I leant back and went'smack'with my leg, kicked him on the side of his face. I kicked again and snapped the indicator off his steering wheel. Frankie went mental. He started driving like a lunatic and hitting me at the same time. I couldn't get out of the car, he was going too fast. We got to an industrial estate and he dragged me out of the car and beat me up properly. He put me back in the car and drove me to my mum's house. He knocked on the door, threw me on the doorstep, and left. Mum was so frightened by all the blood, she couldn't even pick me up. She put me in her car and took me to hospital.

I had a broken nose, and the best pair of black eyes you've ever seen. I didn't hear from him for two months after that, and then he turned up in Wickford again, said he was sorry and he loved me, and I took him back again.

He took me back to Holland, to a birthday party for a friend of one of the brothers. Everyone looked in absolute shock when we walked in. There was a bit of a weird atmosphere all night too – a couple of people didn't even come and speak to him. I picked up on it but I didn't take much notice. We left the party and got on a big coach and went to a nightclub. In the toilets, I got chatting to the main man's wife, Jo-Jo, and she said, 'I've got to tell you something.'

'What?'

'He brought his wife here.'

'You're joking. He's split up from her.'

'No, he ain't. He took her on holiday to Jamaica.' She told me everything.

Frankie was still with her. He was doing the dirty on both

of us. She was the poor little clueless wife, but so was I. He would tell her he was working away and come and be with me for three or four weeks at a time. And then every time he disappeared on me, he was going back to her.

I didn't know what to do with myself. He'd been seeing her all the time, she'd been on my holiday to Jamaica, and now I was stuck out in Holland. How could I have not known what was going on? I came out of the toilets and my blood was boiling. I'd said to Jo-Jo that I wouldn't say anything to Frankie that night, but I couldn't keep it in. I went up to him and said, 'Have you got anything to tell me?' He said, 'I don't know what you're on about.' And I just went SMACK and hit him in the face.

All the main men there were on my side. They didn't like what he'd done. Because especially in those circles, you don't upset the girlfriend and the wife, because they're the ones that can put you in trouble. One of them said to him, 'You might as well go, Frankie. You're not really welcome here, are you?' And the main man and Jo-Jo took me to the hotel to get my stuff and then back to their flat and I stayed there for the whole duration.

I went back on the flight with him but as far as I was concerned it was over.

Three days later, I got a call to say he'd been nicked. And the reason he got nicked was – just like he was playing with two women, he was playing with two drugs teams. Which is a real no-no, a really bad thing, you never do that. Because if you get caught on one team, you lead the police to the other one.

What he'd done is ... the drugs team I knew of, they had a big Magnum lorry that they had had specially customised. It had a private compartment built into it, between the cab and actual lorry, big enough for the driver to get into, and they used to put the drugs in there in Holland. Cost them £40,000. And Customs never found this compartment. There had even been times the lorry had been taken into the Customs shed with the dogs and that, and the dogs couldn't even smell it – it was unbelievable. So they got very confident then. They knew they could send over whatever they liked and it would never be found.

But Frankie took this lorry and showed it to the other drugs team he was working for. And then this other team had a Magnum lorry customised for them as well. By the same person. Well, they didn't know it, but this other team was being followed by Customs at the time. Customs let the lorry come through and followed it. They waited for Frankie to actually get in the hole, in the private compartment, and that's when they went *knock, knock, knock* – caught him in there red-handed. They would never have found the compartment if they hadn't watched him get in it.

So now, Customs knew what they were looking for. Now they were going to check out every Magnum lorry that came through. So the first drugs team, the people in Holland, couldn't use their lorry anymore. Frankie had fucked it up for all of them, because of his greed.

That changed things for me. Before, I had just been Frankie's girl. Not involved. But these people in Holland were really aggrieved. They couldn't get the drugs into the country in the normal way now, because Frankie had blown that, and they told me I had to help them out.

I didn't want to, and I told them that, but they weren't interested. Frankie had got nicked and they knew that I knew all the contacts, and how he used to do it. I didn't really feel like I had a choice. It wasn't a choice – it was more like an order.

So I got involved. I started moving money for them. I had to give up my carer's job, because I couldn't do both.

I had to go round to five or six different people's houses on my own, some of them I knew, some of them I didn't. I had to collect money from them that they owed for the drugs, and count it to make sure it was all right. Counting that much money takes a long time. When I had it all, I had to put it in two carrier bags and take it on the train to London – £200,000 in two carrier bags on the train. I had to go to a particular exchange place on Oxford Street, who knew to expect me. I walked in, they opened the side door, and took the bags off me. I went to the local pub round the corner and had some lunch. The exchange place rang me and told me to come back. I went back, they opened the door up again and gave me a little bag. Now that the cash was in hundred-dollar bills it took up a lot less room. I took it home on the train, wrapped it up like a present, with wrapping paper and a big bow. Then I had to go and meet a lorry driver and give him the parcel, and his job was to put it in his cab and drive it over to Holland. These days, they've got dogs that sniff out money, and they know to look at presents, but in those days it worked.

I had to do that every two weeks or so.

I had to take it over myself one time. I drove to Holland with £200,000 in my spare tyre.

We rang each other from phone boxes, never mobiles, and we had codes. We spelt things backwards, and we had names for different numbers. A 'nevis' was 700, a 'carpet' was 300, a 'bottle' was 200, 'McGarrett' was 50 (because of *Hawaii Five-0*), a 'bag of sand' was a grand. A kilo was a 'soldier'. The 'eagle has landed' meant that the drugs were in the country. Everyone had nicknames: mine was 'The Queen'. I liked that. So it would be, 'Go and give The Queen a bag of sand plus a nevis.' But the sums I was collecting were a lot more than that – one kilo cost £34,000 to £35,000.

It was strange, being a girl in that game. The other girls I knew of were wives. I wanted their lives, but I didn't. The main guy's wife, Jo-Jo, she didn't want for anything, she was completely kept and always immaculate. She had the best jewellery, he upgraded her Rolex watch every year, make-up, hair extensions, sunbeds, nails, Louis Vuitton make-up bag, purse, bag, bigger bag, luggage, anything she wanted. I used to think, why can't I be like you, instead of working for your old man? Why do I have to be living on my nerves the whole time, and on call the whole time, and looking in my car mirrors and wondering who's ringing my bell, and worrying about my door being kicked in?

But then I'd think – she was working for him too. She was like his servant, his little sex servant, rolling him joints and idolising him 24/7.

I didn't have the sunbeds or the jewellery. But I was

earning nice money. Not amazing, maybe thirty grand over a year, but it was nice to have money for a change without having to work too hard for it. And I was a player and I had respect and I didn't have to answer to anyone. I wasn't just a girlfriend – I was one of them.

14

THE DEAL

The deal I actually got done for – the £4 million drug deal that landed me with a ten-year prison sentence for conspiracy to supply a tonne of cannabis – wasn't supposed to be anything to do with me.

So I was unlucky. But really, I was very lucky. If they'd been watching me a week later and caught me doing what I was supposed to be doing, then I might have got twenty years. If they hadn't caught me on that, they'd have probably caught me on something else even bigger. Because these people in Holland were definitely leading me on to other things. And if they hadn't ever caught me, I'd probably be dead by now.

I try to analyse it all the time. I shouldn't have been there that night. But being there meant I got ten years. And ten years – not three, and not twenty – was what I needed to turn my life around.

*

The people in Holland had a cousin. They'd fallen out with the cousin years earlier because they thought he'd grassed on them, but time had elapsed and the brothers in Holland had decided to forgive and forget and give this cousin another chance. I met this cousin at a big slap-up family weekend, at a hotel by a lake. I'd actually organised the party for the main man's father – I'd been his little runaround, getting the invitations printed, sorting all the flights and that. So I was well in there. I met the cousin, and I didn't like him. He had shaved his head and I could see the reason he'd shaved it was that he was ginger. There was just something about him. I didn't trust him, and I could tell he was a complete waste of space.

The feeling was mutual. The cousin wanted my job but he couldn't have it, and he didn't like the fact that I was a woman, and he didn't like the fact that I was there at the family party.

They were going to let the cousin set up a big puff deal. And I said to the main man, 'I don't want to know. I don't get involved with puff, and I don't want to do anything with him. I don't mind doing what I'm doing, but I don't want to be involved with him.'

'No,' he'd said, 'fair enough. His stuff and your stuff will be completely separate.' Fine.

About a week after I met the cousin at this three-day Dutch party, I got a phone call at home from the main man over in Holland. He was in a real state. 'You've got to help me, you've got to help me.' His dad was in a wheelchair, and his mother was his carer. 'My mum's just dropped down dead and my dad's there on his own, and my kids are there. I'm trying to get the first flight home to England. Please go round and look after my dad, please go there.'

I went to the house and it was in complete turmoil. Everyone was in shock. I stayed there for the whole week, caring for his dad, toileting him, everything. That gave me a big boost in the main man's eyes, which the cousin didn't like at all. The cousin spent the whole time the main man was over in England cooking up his deal. I didn't want to know. Mouthy horrible little ginger shit.

So I was in pretty deep with this family. Then, out of the blue, a few weeks later, the main man rang me again, in another panic. The cousin was in trouble and he needed me to help him out. The story was such a cock-up I didn't want to get involved. But I knew what these people were capable of and I didn't see that I had any other option. I'm still not sure, after all the prison courses I've been on, enhanced thinking skills and that, whether I had any other option. I'm not sure what the consequences would have been if I'd have said no.

The main man told me what had happened. The cousin had agreed to accept a lorry-load of cannabis from Holland, and he was supposed to find somewhere to drive the lorry to, to get it unloaded – they call it a 'slaughter'. Only he'd messed it all up. This cousin had gone to some bloke who had a barn in a little village called Mountnessing, and asked him could he borrow his barn for an hour. To this day I still don't know how the cousin picked this bloke. The bloke had asked him what he needed it for, and the cousin had spilled his guts, told him everything. 'OK,' the bloke had said, 'well, what do you want to give me for it?' The cousin had offered five grand and the bloke had said he'd do it for ten. So the cousin had said he didn't think so, but he'd ask. They had haggled for a few days over the price and eventually the cousin had agreed to pay ten thousand. By which time the bloke had said, 'No, I don't want to do it now.'

The cousin had spent so long going backwards and for-wards with this bloke – and getting nowhere – that he was right up against it for finding somewhere to unload the lorry. He rang up his contact and said, 'Stop the lorry, stop the lorry, I've got nowhere to unload it.'

'Sorry,' said the contact, 'it's left. It's already on its way.'

'No, no, you can't, I've got nowhere for it to go.'

'You'd better do something about it then.'

That was when the waste-of-space cousin rang the main man, and when the main man rang me. 'You've got to help us out,' said the main man. 'This lorry's already en route – we need you to find us a slaughter. You don't have to get involved, just find us a slaughter.' They couldn't let the lorry driver sit anywhere for long because of the tachometers that recorded everything they did. Like a little grass sitting in the front of the cab.

I was just going to have to deal with it.

'All right,' I said, 'what's got to happen?'

'Doors off, take the stuff out, doors back on, move on. An hour tops. The lorry driver can put it down as a rest.' The doors had to come off so they would stay bonded. It would look like the bond on the doors hadn't been broken, because we'd have lifted both doors right off.

'How long have I got?'

'You've got until tomorrow morning, nine o'clock.'

I knew some people and I made some calls. Two boys I knew managed to find somewhere, an industrial estate near Wickford. They would go into a warehouse there and unload it. It was just a normal lorry, no one would take any notice. Happy days – it was sorted and I wasn't going to have to go anywhere near it. I rang the main man back, told him I'd managed to find somewhere, took a sleeping tablet and went to bed.

Two o'clock in the morning, my phone rang. I was deep deep asleep. It was the cousin. 'The lorry's arrived, you'd better get your blokes and all that in place,' he said.

'Don't be so fucking ridiculous, the lorry isn't here.'

'The lorry's here.'

'You're joking, ain't ya? It's two o'clock in the morning. We can't do anything with it at two o'clock in the morning. It's an industrial area, where I've got. It doesn't open until nine o'clock.'

'What are we gonna do, what are we gonna do?' He just started really panicking. He didn't have a clue. As far as I was concerned, I'd done my bit, and he'd fucked it up again. I didn't want anything more to do with it. But he was in a complete state.

'Why's it here early?' I wanted to know.

'I don't know, it just is.'

'He's going to have to wait.'

'He can't wait. He's got to be at his delivery spot early in the morning.'

'What are we going to do then?'

'I don't know, I don't know. We're going to have to go and meet him.'

'No, I'm not coming. I'm not coming anywhere. Why do I have to come?' What did it have to do with me?

'If you don't go, I'm not going.'

'Oh, for God's sake. All right then.' I still don't really know what the point was supposed to be of me going there. I think it was that he wanted to offload the responsibility for his fuck-up. He wanted to be the big man, with his big drug deal, but in the end he didn't have the minerals to do it.

I got in my car, and I drove from Wickford, where I was living in my house, to the B&Q on the A12 at Gallow's Corner. I was checking behind me, like I always did these days. Didn't see anything.

The cousin was there in the B&Q car park, and my two boys from Wickford. And, parked a little way away, the lorry. The cousin got out of his car, got into mine, and we drove through the car park over to the lorry. The cousin got out and spoke to one of the lorry drivers.

We drove back to where the boys were waiting. I said to them, 'We haven't got the slaughter; you're going to have to do it on the side of the road, that's all we can do.' These two boys knew a lay-by that was surrounded by bushes and they thought it would only take ten minutes. So the boys drove off in their van, with the lorry following. They were going to unload the lorry in the lay-by, take off what was meant for us, put it in their van and drive off with it. The cousin stayed in my car and we drove off too.

What was I doing driving around Romford with this useless piece of shit at three o'clock in the morning? I didn't want to be anywhere near the lorry, and I needed a fag, so I pulled off in a petrol station nearby. Still checking my mirrors. Still not seeing anything. I got out of the car, and the cousin got out of the car. He was just walking around the forecourt all jittery.

I went over to the little garage shop and bought my fags. As I walked back to get into the car, a car screeched up to me, felt like a hundred mile an hour, and a bloke jumped out and pointed a gun at me. 'Put your hands on your head!' he screamed. 'Put your hands on your head, you're under arrest.' I've never been so frightened in my life. I froze. Then I started shaking. I managed to find some words.

'What for?'

'Tracy Mackness, you're under arrest for importation of a controlled drug.'

I looked around and I couldn't see the cousin. He'd managed to run off. I was on my own, just me and the screaming man with the gun.

'I don't know what you're on about,' I managed to say. 'I haven't done anything.'

And then all hell was let loose. Suddenly, about fifty police were all over this petrol station, coming from everywhere in more and more cars, all plain clothes with padded jackets, all shouting and screaming, all just for me. I couldn't really understand what was happening. And I felt like it wasn't really happening at all, like it was some big nightmare that I was going to wake up from.

I was read my rights, and put in the back of the car. They drove me round to where the lorry was. They'd raided the lorry at the same time. Major operation, National Crime

Squad, eighteen unmarked cars, a hundred police. I sat in the back of the car, in the middle of the night, watching the police unload the lorry.

And at that moment I thought to myself, if I could give every single thing I own to make this go away, I would do it. I knew that in that moment, my life had changed.

15

THE TRIAL

'What's on that lorry, Tracy?'

'I don't know.'

'What's on the lorry, Tracy?'

I was in the back of the police car, watching the lorry being unloaded. There were plain-clothes police swarming everywhere. The two lorry drivers, my two boys, and some other bloke they'd got involved, were all in the backs of different cars, watching the same thing. I had to think quickly. I didn't know what they might find on that lorry. I'd already served one sentence, and I was on bail for another silly thing. This could be really bad for me. If I don't say what I know, and they find cocaine, I could be looking at twenty-five years. So I told them. I'm nicked anyway, I might as well make life easy for myself. Right?

'There's puff on there, I know there's puff on there.'

'How much?'

'Five hundred kilos. Half a tonne. But it's not mine, it's got nothing to do with me.'

A police officer came and tapped on the window and said something into the ear of the one in the car with me. He nodded and the other police officer went off round to one of the other cars.

'Right. Well, we found a tonne on there, Tracy. And now the lorry's going to Dover, to go through the machine to see if there's anything else on it.'

If I was frightened before, I was absolutely shitting it now. I only knew about the 500 kilos of puff. But there must have been another half a tonne on there for someone else to unload. Which meant now we were going to get done for the whole tonne. And if they'd done that, I didn't know what else they might have done. There could easily be 30 kilos of cocaine on there too, anything at all.

We were all taken to Harlow police station. It was probably still only about four o'clock in the morning, maybe five. Everything had happened so fast.

I was taken up to the desk for them to take all my details, do my property, search me, take my jewellery, the laces out of my shoes, anything else I could do any damage with. And that was the first time I saw the others. The cousin was there too by this point, the police had sent the dogs out and got him.

We all stood there looking at each other, in a daze, trying to make sense of it. I knew the two boys and the cousin, but I didn't know their mate, and I didn't know the two lorry drivers. The cousin knew the lorry drivers and me, but he didn't know any of the boys. And we were all supposed to be in a conspiracy together.

There were all grown men, but they looked like a load of frightened rabbits. Everyone just had fear written on their face. And then there was me, a woman with all these men.

We were all strip-searched and put in different cells, so we couldn't talk to each other and sort our stories out. I was still in suspense. I still didn't know what they were going to find on that lorry.

We were in the police station, being questioned, all that night and all the next day and night. All the others went 'no comment' for two days. After my solicitor arrived, I went 'no comment' for two days too. Kept getting brought out, and brought out, and brought out, but I wasn't saying anything else. But I'd already admitted it in the police car, and that made me guilty. And the police told the others that I'd admitted it and told them that that made them guilty.

Then they obviously decided not to keep us any longer. There was nothing else on the lorry. And as far as they were concerned, even without us talking, they had more than enough to charge us.

I was sent to Highpoint Prison in Suffolk, on remand, while we waited for the trial. There was no question of bail. I was on remand for a whole year, and that was a year of hell. It was the constant getting my hopes up, and the constant disappointments, and the constant aggravation. And I hated myself.

I had a visit from my solicitor every week. The charge was conspiracy to supply cannabis, which carries a really big sentence. My lawyers were really worried; they were trying to impress on me how serious it was, especially for me, because of my record. And also because I was already on bail for this other thing. When I'd been with Frankie Farrell, I'd delivered a kilo of puff for them one time. I didn't normally do it, it was a one-off thing, someone needed it as a sample. I went in the car with someone else, over to Crawley, and he got pulled up for speeding and they found the kilo. I had already gone 'guilty' on that thinking I would get a community sentence, or six months maximum, of which I would have only done two. No problem, I can handle that. But now I'd been caught for the same thing while I was out on bail. It looked really bad.

I had to come up with some kind of defence. I couldn't go 'not guilty' because of what I'd said in the police car. And I couldn't just say nothing in my defence. I decided to say that I'd done it under duress. Which I had really, but to run a defence of duress, you have to convince the jury your life was in danger, or the life of your loved ones. Trying to keep that story together was another nightmare. Another time – not that there's ever going to be another time – I would just go 'guilty'. It isn't worth the aggravation – and the getting your hopes up – and I probably would have got six years if I'd gone 'guilty'.

And every two weeks, and then every month, we'd have to go back to court for another hearing.

The trial finally started in October 2002. I'd been on remand since the February. It was a big three-month dog-eat-dog trial, with everyone trying to blame everyone else. It was a serious set-up, with the prosecution and seven sets of defence lawyers, one for each of us.

Those three months were horrendous. The trial was in Chelmsford, and I was on remand in Highpoint in Suffolk. It was a two-hour journey and I had to go backwards and forwards in the sweatbox every day for three months. The sweatbox is a big van with lots of little blacked-out windows down the side. The main door is at the back and when you step up through the door and into the van, you step into a little corridor, a walkway about a foot wide, maybe eighteen inches. There are little doors on each side of the walkway, and the officers open up a door and put you in a little tiny cell, and they lock the door. The outside windows are blacked out but the doors have window panels in them so you can look through and see the person opposite you, across the walkway. I don't travel very well in cars and I got special permission to suck peppermints in the sweatbox to stop me being sick. They're not allowed to stop or to open the doors while the van is in transit, in case people try to get out. It's happened. So when I was sick, it was tough shit.

Some days I left the prison at five in the morning and didn't get back until eight at night. Because even if court only started at nine o'clock, you'd have to make lots of stops at other prisons and police stations to pick up other people. Other days I was so late getting back I got locked out of the prison and they had to find me a police cell to spend the night in. And every day, on the way out of the prison, and on the way back in again, I was strip-searched, and everything I had on me was logged and written down.

Once I was there, I'd be put in a cell down below the court and my solicitor would come to see me. The officers there were Group 4, really friendly, all first names, and they would get me a cup of tea and give me a packed lunch. I lived on crisps for those three months.

For me, that year on remand, and the trial, were harder than all the rest of the time I did. Because of the going to and fro every day. And because I was always getting my hopes up and then getting disappointed. And because of the atmosphere between all of the defendants: none of us was talking to each other. And because the whole time, no one believes you, you're treated as a liar, as something that someone's just walked in, off their shoes. The prosecution are saying, 'You're lying, you're lying,' and you start to believe it yourself, even about the things that are true.

My mum was there every day, and Sam, and my aunties, Janet and Gladys, and Gladys's husband, Bob. My dad didn't come at all. He was ashamed I think, and angry. He'd always told me not to get into drugs, and that if I did I could live with the consequences. I wasn't getting no sympathy from him. He was from that generation. They thought ducking and diving and handling stolen goods and all that was all right, but they didn't hold with getting involved in drugs. Dad would say, 'I'd be a rich man if I'd gone down that line, but I didn't.'

The whole story came out during the trial – the prosecution pretty much nailed it. The bloke with the barn, who had said he wanted ten grand for the cousin to use it, and then decided he wasn't interested, had gone straight to the police. So the police had been watching the cousin and following him for the whole time after that, for ten days. They'd sat outside his house for ten days, they'd followed him to Stansted and seen him get on a flight to Holland, they'd followed him to Holland and seen him meet with someone in a hotel, and they'd followed him back home again. Four cars following him down the M25 at three o'clock in the morning when there's no other traffic – how could he have not clocked them? When the police said that in court, all the rest of us were just looking at him, like – how did that happen, you twat?

So that night, the police sitting outside his house saw the lights go off at ten o'clock. And then the lights came back on, at one o'clock. When he'd left his house an hour later, the police had followed him to the lorry, stayed with him to the B&Q car park, watched me come along, watched him get in my car, and then half of them followed the boys to the lorry and the other half followed my car to the petrol station. I never saw anything behind me but they were there.

The prosecution had the phone technicians in to go through all our phone records; they went through the lot, who'd phoned who. They had the tacograph people to talk about the lorry and when it left and when it stopped and how long it stopped for. They even had CCTV of boxes being loaded on at an Amstrad factory in Holland, although they couldn't prove that there was drugs in them. They knew it, they just couldn't prove it.

Then we each gave our defence, each of the seven of us.

The cousin said he didn't know what was in the boxes. The Dutchmen, the two lorry drivers, had this ridiculous story. Their story was – they were stopped on the motorway that morning by another lorry that had broken down. They'd stopped to assist their fellow Dutchman and he'd said could they do him a favour, could they take these boxes some-where? It was laughable, but what else could they say? The two boys from Wickford, and their bloke, they said they didn't know what was on the lorry, they said I'd asked them to pick something up from the lorry and they thought it was going to be building materials. I backed them up on that, because everyone gets a copy of everyone else's statement before the trial begins.

As for me, well, I couldn't claim I didn't know what was on there. It was looking bad for me.

Our judge in Chelmsford, John Greenwood, was the worst one I could have had. He was known as the 'hanging judge'. He hated drugs, and he had no time whatsoever for me.

The jury were all middle class, because the trial was in Chelmsford. I wasn't happy about that. I'd have had a better chance with a Basildon jury, with working-class people like me.

The cousin came on the stand and said I was the number one. When you get done for conspiracy, they try to work out who was most responsible, down to who was the least responsible, and they charge you in that order. When we'd first been charged, the cousin had been indicted number one and I'd been number two. The lorry driver was three, his mate was four, my boys were five and six, and their bloke that they'd employed was seven. In court, the cousin tried to convince them I should be number one. So he spilt everything he could. He told the court how he'd met me at a big party in Holland, how my nickname was The Queen, how I'd been doing this for years. Because he'd gone over to Holland, and I hadn't, they decided to keep him at number one. But I was number two, and now he'd put all this other stuff in their minds about me.

My duress defence didn't stand up very well. The prosecution said why didn't you just go to the police? And there was another big paper trail and the prosecution found all sorts of bills and made up a big story about me.

And the prosecution played up what a big-time operation this was. Because bits of it were quite sophisticated. Like the drugs had been sealed into computer boxes at the Amstrad depot in Holland. And it all came out too about how the lorry had been bonded, and we'd worked out how to get the lorry unloaded without breaking the bond.

We all went 'not guilty'.

And somehow, despite everything that had happened in the trial, by the time it came to the verdicts, two days before Christmas, I had got my hopes up again.

I could tell the jury didn't like the cousin, and I was hoping they'd come down on him and find me 'not guilty'. I had it in my head that I wasn't going to prison, that I was going home for Christmas.

The verdicts came back. Cousin – 'guilty'. Me – 'guilty'. Lorry driver and his mate – 'guilty'. The two boys from Wickford and their mate got acquitted.

'Guilty' was a blow. But you still hope. In his summing up, the judge said he was convinced I had only known about the half tonne, that I hadn't known about the other half. So I was thinking – he thinks I only knew about half of it, he's only going to sentence me on half.

The judge started dishing out the sentences straight away.

No six-week break for reports or anything. He started with the cousin, and he gave him twelve. He gave the two lorry drivers nine each. He left me until last. I was thinking he was going to say six. He turned to me, and he said nine. He gave me nine years. To run consecutively with the one I already had for the kilo of dope, which made ten. He said, 'Tracy Mackness, you claimed to be a foot soldier, but you were more than that. You were more like a colonel. You are a facilitator through and through.' Even though I hadn't actually committed any crime, I was doing things to help other people to commit a crime – that's facilitation, and he got me on that.

It was pandemonium in court. Everybody talking and shouting and screaming at once. My boys were told they could go and they were joyful obviously. The cousin was in uproar – there was no way he could do twelve years. The lorry drivers, they were Dutch, they didn't really understand what was going on. Mum started screaming, the cousin's mum was wailing, my brother was crying, Sam was crying. My barrister was saying we would appeal.

When you get a big sentence like that, you get taken straight back down to the cells. Mum and my brother and Sam came to see me behind the glass but they were all very upset and that made me more upset. Nobody knew what to say. My brother said he was going to miss me, which just made me even worse. I was gutted, I was disappointed, I was confused. I just wanted to get out of there, out of the situation, and be on my own so I could gather my thoughts. Which is what happened – they took me straight back to the prison, Highpoint, where they could watch me properly, and put me back on my depression tablets, in case I tried to kill myself.

16

BIG BIRD

I been in a lot of prisons in my life. I done a lot of time. If you've never been there, you can't imagine it.

They're all laid out different. Holloway had different wings for different kinds of offenders – maternity wing, hospital wing, remand wing – and it was six to a cell and open-plan showers, plus a couple of rooms with baths in. You wouldn't dream of getting in those baths, some of the things I've seen in there.

Cookham Wood was single cell, with bang-up in your cell from eight o'clock in the evening to eight o'clock in the morning, no tellies, nothing.

Highpoint was two to a cell, and it had a spur outside the cells, like a corridor, with twenty cells either side, and a big iron gate at the end. There were two spurs in a block, and three blocks, plus the new prefabs for enhanced prisoners. You could walk along your spur most of the time, but you

couldn't walk outside it except when they unlocked the gate
for two hours a day for association and exercise. Other times,
the screws weren't allowed to open up that gate, no matter
what. Even if there was a fire, even if someone was having a
fit, even if someone was dying, the Governor had to be there
and a certain amount of officers.

They're all laid out different but they all smell the same –
they smell of disinfectant, because you're always cleaning in
prison, mixed with the musty smell of really old blankets and
curtains, and the smells of women who don't wash – urine
and sweat and musk and BO.

And the sounds are the same too. Women shrieking. And
keys rattling on chains. I don't like the sound of keys even
now.

I started off in Highpoint on a spur in a double cell. Me being
me, within four months of being there, I was on the enhanced
house. When you first go into prison, you're basic. If you do
everything you're supposed to, keep your nose clean, you can
become standard, which comes with extra privileges, like you
can spend £7 a week of your own money in the canteen
instead of £5. And then the next rung up is enhanced, with
more privileges again. When you're enhanced, it's a totally
different ball game. Enhanced prisoners lived in the new
prefab block, and we were all in single cells, like little Trav-
elodge rooms, with a little desk and your own shower and
toilet, and a telly in the cell. Having a telly, I couldn't believe
it. Compared with Holloway and Cookham Wood all those
years earlier, it was luxury. I used to say to the other girls, you
don't know you're born, we used to share six to a cell, we

didn't have tellies. We were allowed out a lot longer on enhanced house, and we were allowed to spend more money, £20 a week of our own money. We could have our own plate and mug and knife and fork brought in from home instead of having to use the canteen stuff. We could have our hair coloured or permed for about three quid, by girls training to be hairdressers in the prison. Other prisoners could only have their hair cut.

I was on remand for a year; then after the trial and the sentencing, the next thing was the appeal. It was about nine more months between the sentencing and the preliminary appeal hearing. More hopes raised, more hopes slammed. The judge at the hearing said he could have given me four-teen years and I'd do better to shut up. There's always the chance when you go to appeal that they will increase the sentence, and I know people that's happened to, so I didn't pursue that anymore.

Around the same time I had my confiscation hearing as well. When you get found guilty for drugs, they take you back to court for an asset-confiscation trial. They try to build up a case about how much money you made out of your crime. So that's like another trial again – you're fighting for what you own. They wanted £500,000 off me. That's what they said I'd have made out of the drugs. They'd done it on street value of the whole thing, which would never have been what I would have got. And which I didn't have. I managed to get it down to £108,000 and I had a year to pay it. I had to remortgage my house and my flat – got £50,000 for the flat and £58,000 for the house. When the cheques came through Mum went down to the court in Southend and paid them. I've got the receipt somewhere – I framed it. That was another battle, another headache. No amount of money is worth it to go through that.

Once I'd got my sentence, and decided not to appeal, and the confiscation hearing was over, things were much easier. I had this big horrendous sentence. But the not-knowing was over now. I couldn't be let down or disappointed anymore, nothing worse could happen to me, so it felt like a lot of the worrying and the pressure was off me. I knew what I was doing now, and I just had to work out how I was going to get through it. Get in a routine, stay out of trouble, establish my reputation, work the system.

At first, I was just in shock, numb. That was partly the drugs they put me on to help me get through. They put me straight back on the antidepressants, which just blanked everything out for the first couple of months. Then they started to wean me off them because they don't like you to get too dependent. And then I didn't feel numb anymore, I just hated myself. Being in prison makes you feel like you're nothing, like you're worthless. You've got no rights, you can't make any decisions about your life, you've got no property, you've got nothing at all. Everything is taken away from you. Anything you want, you have to ask for it, fill out a form for it, and the answer's usually no. You learn to live with rejection and people saying 'no'. Can I have a job change? No. Can I have a change of clothes? No. Can I have a visit? No. Your whole life is governed by paper. You're watched all the time, even your phone calls are taped. And there's no escape from it, no getting away. I found it very hard to come to terms with. I struggled, being such a strong character, to suddenly be nothing, locked up like an animal, being told what to do. There were days I literally felt sick to my stomach about being there, days I thought I couldn't carry on. But I didn't have any option.

It was lonely too. No one to share a bed with, for years and years.

And the worst thing of all, the thing that made me feel ill, that I couldn't let myself think about, was knowing that by the time I got out of prison I would be in my forties. I had thought I had lots of time left. Now, I had to resign myself to the fact I was never going to have kids.

I got so that I would talk myself through the days. 'You've got to stop feeling like this, Tracy, sort it out, Tracy, you can do this.' And, 'You done it to yourself, Tracy; you done the crime, you put yourself here.' It helped me to cope with it, telling myself it was me that put myself there. And I developed a mantra to help me through: 'Deal with it. Deal with it. Deal with it.'

Then, one day, soon after I dropped my appeal and accepted I wasn't going home, something changed in my head.

One thing you got a lot of in prison is time. Time to reflect. On who you are, what you've done, and where you've gone wrong. I used to lie awake at night driving myself mad thinking about it all. There are courses to help you too, 'Enhanced Thinking Skills' courses, and I did a lot of those.

I was lying in my bed one night, turning it all over, and it really hit home. I thought, Do you know what, this is as low as it goes, Tracy. You can't get any lower than this. I was embarrassed and shocked about all the things I'd done, that had felt normal, but I could now see weren't normal at all. I remember asking myself: Why didn't I see all this before? But I think when you're in it, and everyone you're with is in it, it's difficult to see what you're doing.

I saw myself that night for what I was. A no-good drug dealer. A failure. And I made a conscious decision that night that I had to do something with myself. I didn't want to be a failure, I wanted to be something. For my own self-respect. I didn't want the life of crime anymore; I didn't want to be always looking over my shoulder; I didn't want to be an old-woman drug dealer. And I definitely didn't want to come back to prison ever again. I'd spent my 30th birthday in prison, and I was going to spend my 40th birthday in prison, and there was no way I was spending my 50th birthday there. I was as low as I could go, but the only way was up.

After that, I still spent my nights lying awake worrying, but now I was worrying about what work I was going to do, what I was going to do for money. I had no qualifications and a criminal record, so it wasn't looking too good, but I had to have hope, I had to have a goal. That's the only way I knew to get through.

So yes, I had to get in my routine, yes, I had to establish my reputation, yes, I had to work the system. But this sentence was going to be different. This sentence, I was going to use my time.

Everything in prison is routines and rules. Once you been in prison, you can't ever forget them. First, there's roll call. You get sick to death of doing roll call. Absolutely does your head in. Roll call happens five times a day, whatever prison you're in. They roll check you in the morning before they open the cell doors, to make sure you're still in there. That happens at the same time in every prison in the country, then they all ring the numbers through to the head office to say that everyone's accounted for. Then what happens next depends on what prison you're in. At Highpoint, we were let out for breakfast and then we went to work. We'd work from nine o'clock until eleven o'clock then go back to be roll counted again. Then we'd go for lunch, which we could eat in the dining room or in our cells, then they banged everyone up after lunch for an hour and a half. Roll check again, then out to work from half past one to half past three. Then bang-up again and roll count again. Out for tea and association from five o'clock until eight o'clock. Eight o'clock at night was the final roll call of the day and everyone in the whole prison system, except in open prisons, was banged up for the night.

The only change to the routine was when something went wrong. If a set of keys went missing, or a knife out of the kitchen, we'd be put on lockdown. Everyone would be banged up until they found whatever it was. Or even if they were just short-staffed, then we'd be banged up from five o'clock.

Then there's strip searches. Every time you have a visitor. And every time you go in or out of the prison. Which was every day for me during my three-month trial, and every day when I was working in the car dealership when I was at Askham Grange.

And then there's rules about everything – about what

money you're allowed to spend, what visits you're allowed to have, what property you're allowed to keep.

Money is a big deal in prison. And because there's not much money, other things become currency. Fags, or phone cards back in the 1990s, or shampoos. When you're on remand, you're allowed to spend what you like – if you've got it. I had money, so I used to go to the canteen and spend £50 on shampoos and things, then sell them to the prisoners who were sentenced. Even later, when I was doing my sentence, I was all right, because I had money on the outside. So I didn't have to ask my mum to sub me £20 spends every week, on top of her paying to come and see me each week. I didn't have to send begging letters like some of them did. If I wanted a new pair of trainers I could just write to Mum and ask her to buy them for me. If I wanted to use Tampax instead of prison-issue tampons, which are the most awful things you've ever seen, I could do that too.

Property is all controlled. To try to stop harassment and intimidation. You have your property card and everything you have has to be on it. If they do a random room search, and find something in your room that isn't on your prop card, you get done for it. Even if it's something really trivial, and even if you say, 'Oh, it's not mine.' We were allowed our own clothes, but only a certain amount – two pairs of shoes, two pairs of pyjamas or nightdresses, one dressing gown, three bottoms, three skirts, two tops, one jumper, one cardigan, one coat, unlimited underwear. It all has to fit in a box. And we were allowed a certain number of books, a radio, a Walkman as it was then and a certain number of tapes. No phones, no DVDs. Notepads, writing paper, envelopes, stamps, we were allowed. I wrote to Mum every single day. She wrote to me too, not every day, but always signed 'your ever loving mum'. And she sent me flowers. I became well known in prison for always getting flowers; if a big bouquet came from Interflora, it would be for me.

Visits were once a week. Every day when you're on remand, and once a fortnight if you're on basic, but every week when you're on enhanced. The visits when I was on remand were very emotional. I used to get upset seeing my family, and cry a lot. Once I was doing my sentence I got more accustomed to it, but it was still a big deal. The day before, I'd start getting excited. Then on the day, you had to get through the morning, and lunch. Visits would be two o'clock until four o'clock. After lunch, I'd be locked up and I'd get myself ready in my best clothes, and I'd start getting worked up. Then I'd be taken down and get strip-searched, and have everything logged that I was wearing. Then I'd sit on a bench with everyone else and wait to be called.

If Mum said she was coming then she was coming. But sometimes a friend would say they were coming and then they wouldn't. That was horrifying; you'd just be sat there on the bench in front of everyone, like being stood up on a date.

The visitors weren't stripped, but they'd have a rub down, and then go through an arch like in an airport, and get the once-over with a wand and be sniffed by dogs.

Me and about thirty other prisoners would sit across a table from our visitors, in a big room with bars on the windows. The prisoners weren't allowed to get up: if I wanted a drink, my visitor had to get it. The prison officers were on you all the time, watching every movement, looking for anything unusual. I've been on visits many a time where they've dragged a girl off when her boyfriend's given her a kiss and passed her drugs. Long kisses aren't allowed. And I've been inside with lots of girls who are in for passing drugs to their boyfriends on a visit.

Mum came every week, and so did Sam. An hour and a half journey each way, and Mum wouldn't go on holiday in case I wouldn't get a visit. Other friends wrote and visited at first but after a while they all forgot about me. My dad came to see me maybe four times in my whole sentence.

I knew from my first sentence what the good jobs were and I made a beeline for them this time. The first job I got was as a wing cleaner, mopping, sweeping and polishing the floors. One of my jobs was diluting the bleach down because they trusted me to do that.

I quickly became a trustee, a trusted prisoner: the officers could see what I was like. I was a model prisoner, basically. Always had been, every prison I was in. Kept myself to myself, didn't talk nonsense, didn't do drugs, and always respectful to the prison officers. They made me one of the prisoners who had to try to keep control on the spur at night because they thought I could handle myself. The young ones would be running around, having water fights in the bathroom at three o'clock in the morning, and I'd have to tell them to calm it down. They thought it was a big joke, all taking drugs. Or someone would turn their music up really loud, and someone else would scream, 'Turn that fucking music down!' It was a nightmare, because there was no escape from it.

Then I got a job in the laundry. I was out of my cell all day, and I had my own little washing machine and tumble dryer. Sorted. Next I got offered a job on the servery, which again was another good little job, because it meant I didn't have to eat the normal crap everyone else had, I could pick and choose. I used to eat a lot of jacket potatoes.

And then I got myself a job in the gym. That was the ultimate.

You're respected as a gym orderly, you're trusted by the officers, and you've got some authority. Like, if they're at it in the gym or in the showers, it's your job to tell the lesbians to cut it out, or to go and tell the gym staff, 'You'd better have a look in there.' You have to be able to handle yourself, to be powerful enough to say it, and not care that they hate you for it. I loved that job.

I was out of my cell all day, getting fit and losing loads of weight, and the gym staff were really good to me.

On Saturdays, the learning disability people would come in, from outside the prison, and we'd play games with them for a few hours, throw the parachute up in the air for them, get them on the trampoline, that kind of thing. On Thursdays, the women with families would have their kids visit and that was held in the gym so they could play with their kids. We'd make drinks and cakes and crisps and sandwiches for them and eat whatever was left over ourselves.

We served drinks to the adult visitors too – that was a trustee's job because visitors could have passed me things. But they knew I wouldn't do anything to jeopardise my position in the gym, the perks were too good.

The best thing was, I had finally found something I might

be able to do on the outside. I decided I was going to work in a gym, teaching step to over-forties. I started training to become a gym instructor and a step aerobics instructor.

I got another job too in the prison – I worked as an insider. There were four of us. We had to go and meet new people as they came into prison on a Friday night. People would come in, have everything taken off them, all their property, and have it logged and put on their prop card. That all took a lot of time for the prison officers. Then they'd have their initial phone call, where they would usually be crying down the phone. And then they'd be passed to me. While the officers were busy logging everyone, I could give the new girls a bit more time. I could tell them what to expect. What their room would be like, what to do at breakfast and lunch. And I'd help them get through that first evening.

A lot of them would say, 'I can't do this,' and it was my job to tell them they could. 'I'm doing ten years, what are you doing? Three months? I've spent longer than that in the canteen queue.' They would say they were worried about bullying, and I'd reassure them. 'You don't get bullied – it's not allowed in here. If you get bullied, you come and tell me, and I'll get it sorted out. I'll tell the officers. You haven't got to do it, I'll do it for you.' I was a friendly face for them. Because a lot of them are thinking about doing some harm to themselves that first night. And then the next day I'd be taken by the officers to see them in their room and sit and talk to them.

I did loads of other courses in prison, not just aerobics and step. The only learning I did on my first sentence was learning new scams, but I did fifty-three courses in Highpoint and I've kept all my certificates. I did money management, budgeting, RE, computer courses, assertiveness, stress management. I couldn't get enough of it – my brain felt like a sponge. I thought, why didn't I do this years ago? Then I could have made something of myself, been a lawyer or something. And I did two Alpha courses – courses that teach you about the Bible. I liked the course so much I did it twice. I loved going to the Pentecostal church, not just because it was time out of my cell and a chance to get tarted up, I really wanted to go. I liked the music, and meeting the different people, and the testimonies inspired me a bit. I did it because I wanted to do it, not because of what it could get me.

I trained to become a Samaritan too. In prison, you don't listen on the phone, you do it face to face, in someone's cell, for up to four hours at a time. Which is quite scary. Some of the stories you hear, you wouldn't believe, they are really terrifying. Crimes people have committed, or terrible things that have been done to them when they were children. I could get pulled out of my cell day or night to go and listen.

I had learnt the last time I was in prison that you have to not show fear. If you show people you're not bothered, they stay away from you. So the persona came back out – the stand-offishness, the abruptness, the one-word answers. People used to try to talk to me, but I didn't want to know. And for whatever reason, no one pushed me on it, no one ever came up and asked me, 'What's your problem?' They knew I was in there for big bird, they knew it was for a lot of drugs, so I must have connections. I think I frightened them as much as they frightened me.

I was quite happy for the girls, and the officers, to be a bit wary of me, to have that little bit of doubt about what I might be capable of. In that regard it didn't do me any harm that I made friends with Linda Calvey. Linda was quite a notorious figure, and she was in for life, for murder, which she was always adamant she didn't do. Linda was always talking about her solicitor and her appeal.

When I was on remand and put on enhanced house, I was put opposite Linda and that's how I met her. I was moving my stuff over, and she came over and said hello and introduced herself. After that we became mates and we were in and out of each other's cells. It was Linda who got me my first job, in the laundry. She got me the job knowing full well that I would look after her and do whatever she wanted. I used to do her knickers and bras for her, when really they should have gone in with everyone else's once a week. Then she got me the servery job, which was where she worked too. I remember one Christmas Day, we made ourselves sick eating a whole trifle. We gave everyone else a smaller bit so we could have a whole one between us. We were up to no good, but only in little ways like that.

I liked Linda. She managed to keep herself normal, not to go mad, despite having a massive sentence. It was me that persuaded her she had to do some courses, and she had to show some remorse, and comply with the system, if she wanted to get parole. I used to say to her, there's no point fighting the system, you're never going to beat them, they're always going to win. She ended up in an open prison with me, and she's been out now for about three years.

Anne Trigwell was another one I used to hang around

with; she died in prison, of cancer, still saying she hadn't paid two hitmen to murder her third husband. Me, Linda and Anne. Prison aristocracy we were.

I avoided nearly everyone else though.

The junkies were bottom of the pile. All skinny, with no teeth, and wrinkles, because the drugs have ruined them. They were mostly in for dealing small amounts of drugs, or for prostitution or shoplifting that they'd done to feed their habits.

The YOs, young offenders. They're a nightmare because they think it's all a big joke and they've got no respect; they're not frightened of the officers, they don't care about anything. They're up to no good all the time.

The people on remand for really big crimes. The people that have been sentenced and are waiting to be allocated. The mental crew, people with psychiatric problems who shouldn't be there at all. The yo-yos, in and out five or six times during my one sentence. The drug mules, who tend to be black and doing really big sentences. To me they were divs – who wants to strap cocaine to your body or put it in your suitcase? That was just stupid.

I didn't really want to know any of them. I'd talk to them and listen to them in my insider job, and I wanted to help them if I could. I felt compassion for them but I can't really say I liked them.

And Myra Hindley was there in Highpoint too, when I was there on remand. She'd been at Cookham Wood when I was there ten years earlier, and now she was here. She had her own section in the segregation unit, two cells put together, with all her own stuff, rugs and pictures and bits and pieces.

I never went in there but I was told. Only certain prisoners
were allowed to go in, and only certain officers too, ones they
knew wouldn't cause her any harm or try to sell a story to the
papers. Linda used to go in and cut and dye her hair for her;
someone else used to cut her toenails. You never saw her at
Highpoint – it was too dangerous for her to come out and
she'd become like a recluse. Myra Hindley died during my
trial. I remember being driven back in the sweatbox and hearing on the news that she had died in Highpoint Prison. When
we got to the gates there were film crews outside in a frenzy.

There was a lot of lesbian activity in Highpoint. It never
crossed my mind, but I did understand why people did it,
girls who weren't lesbians on the out, who had husbands
and children. They call it 'prison bent'. If you're in there for a
long time, it beats the loneliness, and it's something to do. I'd
say at Highpoint, 50 per cent of the girls were involved,
maybe more. Less than in Askham Grange where they were
all at it, but more than in Holloway, because in Holloway
they didn't really allow it and we were banged up a lot of the
time. It was easy for them in Highpoint because of the layout
of the prison. At night, they locked the main gate up so you
couldn't get out of the spur, but then everyone had their own
key to their cell. So people could intermingle up and down
the corridor, go in the showers, and even let people into their
rooms if they wanted to. It was against the rules: the rules
said no lesbian activity, and if you were in someone else's cell
you had to have both feet on the floor. But there was no
control at night inside the spur – it was the lunatics running
the asylum.

I found it part amusing, part disgusting. It made me laugh how childish it all was, like kids playing games. 'Oh, I really fancy you' – and sending each other love letters and all that. And arguing over birds like at school. Grown women, arguing over a bloke that's really a bird with her hair cut short. There was a big black bloke lesbian at Highpoint called Bigga; it must have been six-foot-four tall, like a basketball player. I say 'it' because that's all you can describe it as. This Bigga had been chucked out of Holloway because she was causing too much trouble, and now she hit Highpoint, with her reputation following her. She didn't waste any time getting down to business. Within two days she had about five different birds in tow and they were all fighting over her, physically fighting – 'You was with her last night, she should be with me tonight.' Pathetic.

It was disgusting too. They'd all walk around with big love bites where they'd been sucking on each other during the night. They loved it showing. And they'd all get diseases from each other, big cold sores where they'd been going down on each other, because there was lots of swapping.

And like in every prison there was the low-level constant harassment everyone gets when they first come in. People constantly pestering you – 'Have you got a fag? Have you got tobacco?' Have you got this, have you got that? All day long. A lot of these girls are off the streets, in there for prostitution or drugs or shoplifting. You got to put a stop to that quick. Otherwise, the people running it start thinking they can tax you, bully you, into giving them your things.

The job I did, the insider job, helped stop the bullying,

because people knew the likes of me had our ears to the ground and would hear about it. But you always had people who would try it. Usually people with no money and no means of getting any sent in. The prison came down really hard on it. They did not suffer it at all; if they heard about it, you were nicked.

While I was at Highpoint a group of girls rioted for two days and smashed up a whole block. I don't know to this day what it was about. It wasn't my block, but I could look out of my window and see them trashing everything, throwing their beds out. They had to get the army in to disperse them in the end. I remember looking out of my window and seeing two members of the army escorting each woman. About eighty of them. They were all shipped off to different places round the country, far away from their families, as a punishment. What a stupid thing to do.

I always met my sentence plan. When you first get sentenced, you have to go in front of a board. And on that board is the Governor, your probation officer, your personal officer, someone from healthcare. Everyone sits around and draws up a package for you; they decide what you have to do throughout your sentence – what courses, what job, what behaviours. And every year you go back in front of the sentence planning board and they look and see what you've done out of what they asked you to do. Well, every year, I'd done it all. It suited me quite well, having that structure and no distractions, and I knew how to play the system, get everyone on my side. My reports were always blinding. From the gym staff, from the officers, the people who trained me to be a Samaritan, everyone. Great, bully for me.

I felt settled at Highpoint; I was quite happy. I had my own cell, my visits once a week, my job in the gym. I'd got everything how I wanted it and I was doing my sentence the best way I possibly could.

17

BIDDY AND ME

They never tell you when you're being transferred until the day. It's supposed to be for security reasons. That never made much sense to me especially if you're going to an open prison anyway, but those are the prison rules – that's just how it is. So I knew I was going but I didn't know when. Then it came: 'Tracy, pack your stuff, you're going.' One hour later, no goodbyes, I'm gone.

The day you move to an open prison is a day in your sentence you never forget. It's exciting, because it's the final chapter, the last move. Open prison is where they prepare you for living in the outside world again, make sure you're ready. But it's unsettling too.

I did want to get to the open prison, because I knew that was the fastest way through my time. I'd worked hard to get there, sussing out the system, even telling a few little fibs on my application form. At the same time, I didn't want to go, I was dreading it. I liked it where I was – I had my whole life mapped out and sorted there. I was out of my cell all the time, doing my gym courses, running my step classes, keeping super-fit, all day until eight o'clock at night when everyone gets banged up. I had my routine and my friends, I knew what I was doing, the staff were good to me, no one bothered me. Going to open prison, you have to start again. You aren't known, you aren't respected, you don't know what it's going to be like. Really, I didn't want the change.

Also, in closed prison you get your own cell. I'd got used to my own company and I liked it. I knew in open prison it would be ten, twelve girls in a dorm, with the new arrival getting the worst bed that no one else wanted. I knew what the dorm would be like – great big Jamaican yardie girls kissing their teeth and coming naked out of the shower and creaming themselves right in front of you; everyone playing their music loud; arguing about what to watch on the telly; gossiping and bitching about the smallest, made-up thing; all PMT-ing at the same time. Nightmare.

So I would have preferred to do all my time in a closed prison, but you can't. They got you there really.

East Sutton Park, an open prison in Kent. I knew it was going to be a big culture shock. I'd braced myself for it, told myself I had to like it, because I was going to be there for a long time – three years. Usually only lifers do that long in an open prison, but they'd let me because I had such a long sentence, and I was a model prisoner. I'd done everything they asked and the sun shone out of me as far as they were concerned.

I knew a girl who was already there – Louise, who I'd been in prison with before. It was funny we were friends because she wasn't really my type of person. She was a high-flyer with a phone company who'd got four years for corporate fraud. She'd run up about £500,000 on the company credit card. And she was a bit of a cry baby, a daddy's girl, even though she was about the same age as me. She used to talk in a little-girl voice and throw tantrums and get what she wanted that way. Anyway, we were friends, and it was handy, because Louise came to the gate to meet me. She was pleased to see me, showed me round, introduced me to everyone. That helped, being shown round rather than having to find my own way.

The prison itself looked completely different from Highpoint. From the outside, it didn't really look like a prison at all, more like a stately home, a big manor house. Looking at it, I thought, This might be all right. But then inside, it was mostly just the usual clinical corridors and noisy smelly dorm rooms. The dining hall, though, they'd had to leave – it was a listed building, so it had the original old oak beams. Reception too, and some of the offices, so you got strip-searched under sixteenth-century oak beams. The beams didn't make it any less degrading having someone tell you to take all your clothes off though. I never got used to that.

So I'd got there, been strip-searched, been shown around by Louise, been shown my bed – the bed in the biggest dorm and in the horrible-est, tiniest corner, with no space so all my stuff had to go under the bed.

And then the prison staff had my application form that I'd

filled in to get there. The little white lies I'd told on the form about having experience with animals had worked – I'd got accepted onto the open prison straight away. And now they were saying, 'Oh, work-wise, it says here you want to go and work on the farm. We'll show you round.'

The farm was a little way away from the prison, about five hundred yards. I was feeling pretty apprehensive as we walked down the path towards it. The first thing that hit me was the smell. It was horrendous. Pig shit smells awful. Just awful. And I thought, Aaagghhhh, I don't know if I can deal with this. My mantra, which I'd learnt on an Enhanced Thinking Skills course, to get me through every day, every difficult thing in prison, was 'Deal with it'. But I didn't think I could deal with this.

And then they showed me the pens. In each pen was a massive sow, and each sow had loads of babies. Most of the sows were just lying there on their sides, not moving, with the babies all on them, getting milk. I said, 'So what do you have to do?' And they said, 'You have to feed them and clean them out.' I wasn't just apprehensive now, I was really scared.

And then that's when I saw Biddy. As we were walking around, we turned a corner, and there was this pig there. Just her, standing all on her own. I looked at her, and she looked at me. She had these sad big eyes, really expressive. And something just clicked. There was a connection there. I felt a bit choked up, for her and for me. And I just thought, I want to do this. I want to come and look after you. If I can't do it, I can't do it, but I'm going to give it my best shot. Love at first sight.

*

The next day I couldn't wait to get over there to see her, to see Biddy. I got my green overalls, and my induction talk, and off I went.

Pretty soon I had my new routine all mapped out.

The night officers would wake me up at five o'clock in the morning so I could go and use the gym. I'd go back on the house, have a shower, get changed, and be at my farm job at eight o'clock.

The little team of farm girls would meet together with Mrs Coveney – she ran the prison farm – first thing, have a cup of tea, and she would tell us what we were doing that day. The mornings were always spent feeding the pigs, and cleaning them out. Each girl would get her own section. Afternoons we'd do little jobs around the farm – mending gates, moving sheep around, cutting the hay, things like that – and we'd feed the pigs again.

It was hard physical work. I would leap over into the pen, with my pig board, to protect me from any attacking pigs, and to move the pigs around with; then I'd scrape all the muck from the pen out through the archway; and then leap over again into the next pen. By the time you'd done ten pens, you'd have a whole high-sided trailer full of muck. It was like a workout in itself. And some of the pigs could get nasty, come running at you, barking like a dog, especially the sows protecting their babies if they thought you were going anywhere near them. I took some nasty nips, and one time a girl got three inches of boar tusk in her leg. But I loved it. When I was working on the farm, in with the pigs or out in the fields, I didn't feel like I was in prison. It took me away from where I was. It became my whole life. I stopped noticing the smell after a couple of days.

I got more and more involved, and more and more attached to these pigs. I just wanted to give them the best care I could. They always had a clean bed, always clean straw at night; I didn't want them lying in their own mess. And I used to give them more food than I was allowed to. You were supposed to weigh it, but I didn't bother, I did it by eye. I used to get it in the bucket, and then give them one for luck, so they always got more than they should have.

I used to stop them bullying each other and ill-treating each other too. I couldn't stand to see that. A lot of the boars, they used to bugger each other. It happens. But we noticed one day that all the boars had started picking on this one other pig – they were all just buggering him, made him their bum-boy. Well, I couldn't bear it, I had to get him out. The others were all laughing at me getting so upset, they thought I was mad. But I wasn't having it. I put him in his own little pen, with some of the girls, who weren't going to do it to him.

After a bit, I was allowed to stay over at the farm after the working day had finished, in the evenings and at night, just sitting and chatting to my favourite pigs, or watching babies being born. It was amazing – most of the time they didn't need any help, really. I loved watching that.

Loading them up to be slaughtered, I had to programme myself, in my head. I had to convince myself it was the right thing to do, that that was what they were for, that was what they'd been bred for, and that my job was to look after them as best I could. I could do that fine most of the time except when it was one of my favourite sows that I'd got friendly with. Then I did get really upset.

Within a month Mrs Coveney had seen something in me – she'd noticed how I was going way, way beyond what I had to do. How much I loved the pigs, and how I had taken to them.

Mrs Coveney was about fifty years old. Everyone liked her. She was slim and really nice-looking, with long blonde hair. She didn't have any children of her own but she was a real motherly type. She was always understanding, always had time to listen, and she'd give you advice. Nothing was too much trouble for her; she didn't have a nasty word in her, everything was about you. She and her husband were both prison officers at East Sutton Park. They could have run their own pig farm and made it a proper business – Mrs Coveney knew everything there was to know about pigs, she was a natural, she'd been doing it all her life – but they didn't want that. They had their steady jobs and their nice pensions, and a house in the prison grounds, and their horses to look after. So they were quite happy.

'Yeah,' I said to Mrs Coveney, 'I'm quite enjoying it.'

'Well, why don't you do something constructive while you're in here?'

'Like what?'

'Have you ever thought of an NVQ? We had a girl here once who did level one, a few years ago, but no one else has got involved for a long time.'

I wanted to know what it would involve. I had done a lot of courses in prison, but I had left school without one qualification. For me, the thought of doing an NVQ was really powerful.

'It's everything to do with pigs,' Mrs Coveney said. 'Feeding them, cleaning them, treating them when they're ill, bio-security, infection control, disease control, breeding pro-grammes. Everything. You'll get assignments, and we have to get evidence that you've done everything – photos of you cutting a piglet's teeth, that kind of thing.'

'All right,' I said. 'I'll give it a go.'

'Only,' said Mrs Coveney, 'we'll do levels one and two together for you.'

So that's what I did. For the next nine months I threw myself into it. Completely. It was easy for me, because I was so interested, I wanted to learn. The other girls found it highly amusing; they didn't understand me at all. I read all the books I could; I studied the pig food labels and Sellotaped them into books; I learnt all the injections pigs had to have and how to give them (in the muscle in the back of the leg, which is right near their balls on the boy piglets, and they really scream). I was engrossed, I was just dedicated, it was all I thought about, all I wanted to do. I whizzed through it, did it in nine months when at college it would have taken me fifteen. And because I was not just at college reading books, but on the farm every day with Mrs Coveney, who knew everything from twenty-five years of experience, I learnt so much more. Like how to tell when a pig's about to farrow – you can squeeze one of her teats to see whether her milk's come in, and watch to see when she starts making herself a nest out of her straw – or how to tell when a far-rowing pig's in trouble, and what to do about it. With a pig in trouble – when a piglet had stuck in her uterus – Mrs Coveney showed me how she would administer an injection of oxytocin, to speed up the contractions and make the pig a bit dozy. Then she'd put a big glove on, put her hand inside the pig, and turn the piglet round and pull it out. And then the other piglets just popped out straight after. That was just brilliant, to watch her do that. Within a month, I was doing that too. I passed my NVQ levels one and two no problem.

And then I said I wanted to do level three. Well, no one at the prison had ever done level three, and they had to get the outside assessor in from Hadlow College. And he was really impressed with me; he said he couldn't believe how much I knew. It was good to get that feedback, especially in prison. Good for me, and for Mrs Coveney too.

And then I wanted to do level four. I loved it – I couldn't get enough of it. And once I'd done level four, I knew as much as they did, there was nothing left for them to teach me. I'd mastered it all, no fuss, and it felt like I'd been doing it forever.

18

THE GIGGLY PIG IS BORN

All in all, even though I was in prison, it was a really happy time for me.

It only took me about six months to get the prime spot in a nicer dorm. A corner bed, with a view, and lots of space for all my stuff. Great, I thought, I can sit this out for the next two and a half years now.

I had my routine – there's always routine in prison – but at the same time the farm was a big adventure. Madness, really. Exciting, and not like being in prison. I was learning, I was outside all the time, I was keeping fit. And I was given more and more responsibility, and allowed to spend as long as I wanted there. I remember one day they let me cut the hay – on my own little tractor with a machine on the back. It was sunny and hot and I spent the afternoon driving up and down the fields in a world of my own, just the noise of the machine and no one telling me what to do and for a few hours I forgot where I was. Sometimes I'd be on the farm, on my own, at nine o'clock at night, when everyone else was back in the house. I just loved that, really loved it. It made me feel good about myself.

The staff were good to me; I never had any bother there. At East Sutton Park it was very relaxed; the girls used to be allowed to call the Governor by his first name, but I never did, because for me that wasn't respectful. For me, he was always Mr Carruthers, and Mrs Coveney was always Mrs Coveney. They liked me, and they used to give me special treatment, bent over backwards for me to be honest, because they could see I really wanted to do this, with the pigs. They used to give me swerves too. One time, a girl said I ran her over with a tractor. I hadn't run her over, but I might have run at her. But it was only her word against mine and Mrs Coveney – she took my side. Later on, I used to get all the good little prison jobs too, like working in the charity shop in Maidstone, and doing telesales with little headphones for a window-cleaning firm. Even the Governor's wife, Mrs Carruthers, liked me. She was a prison officer too and every-one was frightened of her in the prison, but I think Mr Carruthers must have talked her into it.

I had a few friends, not many. I didn't need them and to be honest I didn't have a lot in common with a lot of the girls in there. The telly room was just girls arguing about what to watch, and bitching and gossiping and smoking. I'd given up smoking because I couldn't roll and I got sick of having to ask other people to do it for me. Then, a lot of the girls, they weren't right in the head, especially the lifers. Lifers were mostly warped to start with, and then they'd get so institutionalised from being inside so long, they couldn't cope with life on the outside. A lot of them would mess up about a week before they were due out, so they wouldn't have to go. And most of the others – they'd just talk such nonsense. Because inside, you could say anything, and no one knows whether it's true or not. You got no way of knowing. And the ones on drugs, they would just talk about scoring, about how they were going to score on their day off. They had kids, but they were more interested in scoring heroin on their day off than in seeing their kids.

So I didn't talk just to talk, I didn't get involved. People said I was unapproachable and I liked that. Everyone knew not to mess with me. Even the big butch lesbians, they never bothered me there.

So yeah, it was a happy time. But at the same time I was really torn, because I knew I had a decision to make. Because in the meantime, while I was working on the farm, I'd been carrying on with my gym instructor courses as well. I'd been going off with two other girls to a men's prison every day for a month, to get my NVQ level three in step aerobics. I had to decide what I was going to do when I got out. I knew I only had one chance – if I messed it up that would be it. It was weighing very heavy on my mind.

An episode of *Jimmy's Farm*, the BBC One series that was popular at that time, helped me make my decision. Jimmy's boar, Blade, had died of a heart attack in the previous episode, and in this episode they were looking for a new boar. Well, interestingly enough, this women's open prison in Kent breeds these particular kinds of pigs. So they came to

East Sutton Park, and they filmed in the prison foyer, and on the prison farm, and then they asked whether they could film an inmate working on the farm. Usually prisons are reluctant, but I was such a model prisoner that they made an allowance for me; they said it would be all right, I wouldn't show anyone up. So there I was in my green overalls, grinning away, with this lovely little store pig I'd bred. Porridge, they were going to call him. And as they're filming Jimmy loading up Porridge to take him away, Jimmy's chatting to me, about my NVQs and that, and then he offers me a job. I say, 'Yeah, I wouldn't mind.' He says, 'Well, when you get out, come and see me and we'll see what we can do.'

So then I thought, 'OK, that's what I'll do, when I get out I'll go and work for Jimmy on Jimmy's Farm.'

From then on, I was thinking about the future all the time, planning it in my head, lying on my bed. I knew I needed to learn as much as possible. So once I knew everything about working on the farm with the pigs I asked to go and work in the prison's butchery department. The prison farm bred the pigs, the pigs went off to be slaughtered, and then they'd be brought back to the butchery department, where they'd be made into sausages, packed up and sold in the little prison shop or, a couple of times a month, at a farmers' market.

I even managed to get myself on a sausage-making course. This course was being run in the prison butchery department, but by the local college, for outsiders, not prisoners. I asked the Governor, Mr Carruthers, could I go on the course and he said yes, but I'd have to pay, the same as everyone else. It was four hundred quid and I didn't have any money at all then, so I applied to a charity called Women in Prison. It took some hard persuasion down the phone because they'd already paid for all of my gym courses. In the end, the woman said she'd pay for it, but that this was the last course she was going to fund for me. I said that was fine, because I wouldn't ever ask her to pay for any more. Simple as that. So she paid, and I got to go on this course. And I learnt a lot more than anyone else, because when they'd all gone home for the day I was still there. The butcher taking the course – he'd come down from up north so he wasn't going home in the evenings, so he taught me how to cure bacon, hams, gammon, the lot. Lots of added value. So now, I knew it all. And I was going to go and get a job on Jimmy's Farm.

That all changed the day they took me to a farmers' market. Before I went, I didn't even know what a farmers' market was. They had kind of sprung up while I'd been in prison. All I knew was, Mr and Mrs Coveney used to go there once a month to sell sausages, and they used to take two girls from the butchery department with them. I hadn't given it any thought at all until they asked me, did I want to go?

It was really big excitement for me, the chance to go out for the day. And the chance to do something different.

So they took me out to this farmers' market, in a little village called Headcorn. We set up the stall, with the sausages out on the chiller and on the table, and a big banner saying East Sutton Park farm. And I was feeling apprehensive and anxious, to be honest. I couldn't get my head round it that they were going to let me work on the stall, and take customers' money. And I wasn't sure whether the customers would know that we were prisoners. The banner said East

Sutton Park, but did people know that was a prison? As it turned out, lots of them didn't know, until I told them.

And then, when the market opened, I couldn't believe it, it was crazy. The number of customers, and the demand for these products – people were buying loads of packs at a time, it was just mental. I hadn't realised at all what the demand was – and not just for our products, for everything.

Suddenly, I was having a brilliant time. I was in my element. I thought, I know exactly how to do this. I was grinning away, chatting to all the customers – some of them were regulars and said they hadn't seen me before – telling them about myself, how I normally worked on the farm and that, how I'd never been to a farmers' market before, and telling them all about the sausages. And I was talking people into buying more and more packs. And by one o'clock we'd sold out. Usually it would have taken them until three o'clock but because I was there, geeing everyone up and creating a buzz and talking people into buying more and more, we'd sold out by one.

And that was it. I made a decision, right there, at the farmers' market in Headcorn.

I thought, I can do this, I can do this on my own. Why would I want to go and work for Jimmy if I can do this for myself? I'd never been good at working for other people – that had always been part of my problem.

I couldn't wait to get back to the prison so I could start working it all out. I went back to my dorm and lay on my little bed and I thought, This is it, this is what I'm going to do. It just felt completely right, it smelled right. I could see my future.

*

From then on, the passion for the pigs became an obsession. I had no doubt anymore. This was what I was going to do. The pigs took over.

And I realised, although this was a weird thought, not the way you normally think about doing time, that my time in prison was running out. I had to gain as much knowledge as I could, and get as ready as I could, while I was still in prison – while I was being fed and looked after and everything was being done for me – before I had to go out and earn money and do it on my own.

And although I had the basic idea, from what we were doing at the prison, I wanted to do something much bigger, much better. Mr and Mrs Coveney, they only did eight or nine flavours of sausage, they only had one van, they only did a couple of farmers' markets a month. For them it wasn't a real business, it was just something to pay for the pig food on the farm. Me, if I do something, I want to do it to the best of my ability, always. I wanted to do this as well as it could possibly be done, with no fat in the sausages, lots of flavours, lots of vans, lots of markets.

I had eighteen months left on my sentence. Luckily, each bed in the dorm had a little partition, for privacy, so no one could see me as I lay there reading *Farmers Weekly* and *Pig World* and working it all out, every detail – how many pigs I wanted, what kind of land I would need, where the big farmers' markets were, what equipment I was going to need and how much it would all cost.

Once I knew what I needed I had to work out how to get it. First, I had to learn even more: I had to learn how to run my own business. Then, I was going to need pigs, land to put them on, premises to make the sausages in, and money to buy vans and equipment. Somehow – by good luck, by graft, by persuasion, by never taking no for an answer – I managed to get them all. I suppose I have been a manipulator all my life really, I've always known how to play the system, how to get everyone on my side.

They run business studies courses in prison, so I did a couple of them. They didn't really teach me anything much to be honest. And I learnt how to use a computer – because I hadn't ever learnt how to use one before. And I taught myself a lot of bits and pieces, in the library. And then this man came to the prison who wanted to do an exhibition for University of the Arts, London, about prisoners starting their own businesses. I don't know why. He used to come every Monday for about eight or nine weeks. And we each had to write our own business plan, as part of this course. So after talking to him a couple of times I knew what I had to do to write a business plan.

I had about £4000 in savings. You got paid in prison for the work you did, but you couldn't spend it, you had to keep it, save it. The idea was that that would help give you a head start when you got out.

Somehow I persuaded the Governor, Mr Carruthers, to let me use my savings to buy some of his pigs off him. I spent a lot of time thinking about what pigs I wanted and breeding them up.

Then my old friend, my best friend, Sam Clark, agreed to let me use her and her husband's land. Over all these years, she'd always been there to bail me out of whatever trouble I got into, and she was there for me again now.

Sam and her husband, Phil, they had a farm up in Brentwood, near the Brook Street roundabout, junction 28 of the M25. It wasn't a working farm but they had about fifty acres of farmland. And I was always asking Phil, 'When I get out, are you going to let me put pigs on your land?'

And he always said no. 'No,' he said. 'I don't want pigs here, we're right on the M25. It's not happening. No way. I don't want it.' I used to drive him mad asking every time I saw him. And in the end it was getting close to when I was getting out and I must have caught him on a good day because instead of saying no, he said, 'Right, how many are you on about?'

'About thirty,' I said.

'Right, OK then. But I'm telling you now, you've got to put a proper fence up,' he said. 'I don't want them getting on the M25.'

I promised. And, as far as I'm concerned, they never did.

I managed to find premises where I could make the sausages.

During the last year in an open prison, you're allowed out to work, properly, in the community. While I was home visiting my mum one weekend, I saw an advert in a local shop – the shop that I own now. The owner, Len Doolin, was looking for a sixteen- or seventeen-year-old, someone he could train up. He took one look at me and said, 'You're not exactly sixteen, seventeen.' I looked at him, looking like someone's grandad with his great big grey sideburns left over from the Seventies, and said, 'I'm not exactly a trainee either. But I want to learn, and I can probably help you. I can make sausages and you can't.' So he agreed to take me on. And, after he'd promised to tidy up the premises a bit, the prison agreed to let me work there. So I spent the last year of my prison sentence working in Len's shop in Romford, learning, still learning, all the different parts of the trade, and also going out to farmers' markets and starting to put my own plans in place, so that as soon as I got out I'd be able to start up on my own. I even got Len to agree to rent me the back part of his shop, for me to use as premises to make the sausages, with him selling out the front of it.

That was the pigs, the land and the premises. But my £4000 savings that I'd earned in prison were wiped out buying the pigs off the Governor, and paying for a couple of pig huts and an electric fence to stop the pigs getting onto the M25. I didn't really know where I was going to get the rest of the money that I would need.

When I had written my business plan for the man doing the university exhibition, I had said that I was going to go to a bank. But I knew that, in the real world, you couldn't do that. When you come out of prison, you have to declare you've been in, you have a very bad credit rating; you're up against it – no bank is going to lend you money to start a business. You can't even get a bank account, let alone a business loan.

Mum said she'd remortgage her house for me. But she didn't want me to start up straight away. She wanted me to come out and do it slowly slowly. But I knew that if I didn't do it straight away, I might not do it at all, I might slip back into my old ways. I was worried about that. My plan was, I come out, the pigs come out and I'm doing it. So I was a bit stuck.

Then, out of the blue, an old boyfriend got in touch, Paul

Allen. We'd been together when I was eighteen and we'd
kept in touch through the years, on and off. Sometimes we
would go for two or three years without seeing each other,
but we'd always been able to just pick up again.

Paul was a good-looking bloke. Tall, with jet-black hair
from his Italian mother, and a smart dresser. When he
walked into a room, people looked at him. Always had a
flash car. And he was straight as a die, an upright person,
always had a proper job, never into all the mischief I was
into, never been in trouble in his life. He was cocksure of
himself, very opinionated. If he thought you were a bum,
he'd say you're a bum. Back when we'd been together, he
used to say, 'You're going to end up in prison, you are.'

Paul had seen me on telly, when I'd been on *Jimmy's Farm*,
and he'd got in touch with my brother Gary, and said to Gary
to give me his number. So Gary give me his number, and I
rang him up and told him I was still in prison. It was like I'd
just seen him yesterday.

'I'll come on a visit if you want.'

'It don't work like that at this prison,' I said. 'I can go out.'

'I'll take you out for the day then.'

So he came and picked me up and we went to Brighton
for the day, had lunch and all that. He bought a bottle of
champagne, which wasn't allowed. He was the perfect gentleman. And I was telling him about my ideas, what I wanted
to do. And he said, 'Do it – you can do it.' He said, 'But don't
put your mum under pressure, don't borrow from her,
because what if it fails, and she's got no income, to pay back
her mortgage?'

I started seeing Paul every time I was out on home leave.

Nothing very serious. And Paul said he'd help me. He'd lend me the money, and he'd go with me to buy the stuff I needed.

So we went out, and we bought my first little van, my little chiller van – I've still got it now. We bought it from someone he knew. That cost fifteen grand. And we had it sprayed black, and had *Giggly Pig* written on it. Sam had come up with the name – it was me and her, we were the original giggly pigs really, because we were always just making each other laugh. Now my pigs are the giggly pigs though, because they have a good life while they're with me.

And then Paul bought me everything I would need for the market. Tables, a gazebo, the hot plate for the frying pans, ice, everything. And I needed some new equipment too because Len's was all old as the ark, I didn't want it. So Paul took me down to Windsor Food Machinery in Chatham and bought me a little mixer, the smallest one, more like a dough blender really, the one I knew because they had it in prison. And a little mincer, and a little sausage filler. So I was set up. And by the time we'd finished it was about twenty-two grand.

And yes, Paul could have lost all that money. And everyone was telling him not to do it. But he believed in me, and he wanted to help me. And I'd paid him back every penny within a year.

The week before I got out, I went round spraying the pigs I was going to take: thirty pigs in total – two sows that were in pig, due to farrow any minute, a couple of in-pig gilts (gilts are female pigs that haven't had babies yet), one boar, about ten store pigs nearly ready for slaughter, and about twelve little ones that were about eight weeks old. And in my head I was thinking, This has to work. It has to.

19

TRACY THE PIG FARMER

The day I left prison, 26 February 2007, aged forty-two, I had my NVQs level one to four in pig husbandry, thirty pigs and £22,000 in debt from buying the vans and equipment I needed.

From the outset, no one that knew me thought it would work. My mum, my dad, Stella, Sam, my brother, my aunts and uncles, all my mates down the pub, they were all laughing about it. My dad, he'd been in prison, and he knew how many people thought they'd make a change and then never did. And he knew how hard farming was. He was openly mocking me about it. They all thought I'd try it for a little while and then give up and just slip back into my old ways.

But Paul believed in me. And Mrs Coveney, from the prison farm. She told me I could do it. 'Tracy, if anyone can do

it, you can.' And she said if I ever had a problem I could ring
her up. In the early days she used to come and see me too,
not just as a mentor, as a friend.

And the other person who believed it was going to work,
was me. I knew it was going to work, because it had to. And
I knew I had to start straight away, because if I had a week
off, I wouldn't do it.

So when I came out of prison I had one day off, and then
I got back to work. I went back into the prison and got the
pigs out. And then I knew there was no going back – I just
had to get on with it.

For the first weeks I was out, I went a bit on the rampage.
I was free after six years and I was trying to do it all. I had
missed out on so much, I deserved to go out and go mad. So
I was out at pubs, out partying with friends, coming in at five
o'clock and then going to work at six. But after about three
weeks of burning the candle at both ends, I thought, I can't
do this. I just can't. What I used to do years ago, I can't do it
anymore. Mum was really on my case too, moaning on at
me. So I just stopped going out.

While I was still out and about, in those first few weeks, I met
a bloke called Barry down the pub one night. At first I didn't
like him, and he didn't like me. We hated each other in fact.
He used to be all sarcastic in the pub – 'Oh, here she comes,
the sausage baron' and things like that. Then one day, out of
the blue, he asked me out. We moved in together a few
weeks later, in a little rented flat.

My mum could never stand him.

*

With one big exception, the next couple of years were all slog and aggro and grief. I worked long long days, in the vicious, bitter cold and the wet and the dark, with one week rolling into the next. And it was just me, Sam, Barry and my mum in those years – but mostly me – feeding the pigs, mucking them out, making the sausage, and selling it at the markets. There was always something new going wrong. It was chaos most of the time, to tell you the truth. Sometimes, when I was trying to get the pigs into the pen and they wouldn't budge, or when I was making sausage on my own at four o'clock in the morning, I just wanted to lay down and cry.

I remember mornings I would wake up at three o'clock in the morning and it was dark and it was so cold I could see my breath. I'd look out of the window, and see pigs, and mud. I'd get up in the cold, get dressed in the cold, go to work in the cold. I'd come back after an eighteen-hour day and it was dark again and it was still cold.

I admit there were days I wished I could go back to prison for a rest.

But every time I felt like giving up, the pigs saved me. Knowing that they were my responsibility, and I had to get up and look after them every day, kept me on the straight and narrow. Even on Christmas Day, I had to get up and feed them, and then I had to finish my mum's Christmas dinner and get in the car and feed them again.

One major source of grief through that time was what was going on with me and Sam. When I was still in prison, and when I'd just come out, Sam wasn't just letting me keep the pigs on her land, she was helping me with making the sausage and selling at the markets too. When I got out, Sam suggested that we become business partners. I wasn't really keen, because I felt like it was me that had put all the effort in – I'd done my NVQs, I'd done all the research, I was the one who knew about the pigs. Her husband Phil wasn't keen either; he said friends going into business together would end in tears. But Sam really wanted it. And reluctantly I went along with it, because she was my friend, and because I didn't have anywhere else to put the pigs.

Now, looking back, I do realise that I owe a lot to Sam, and to Phil. I couldn't have got started at all without them. And she was doing a lot for the Giggly Pig. And she couldn't put in what I was putting in because with me it was a passion, I was hungry, I had to have it, but with her she had her family to look after and her own demolition business to run.

But back then, really, to me, it felt like she was getting to be a partner but it was still me doing all the work. I was the one getting up at five o'clock in the morning and going round the shop and making all the sausage. Sam did get up early to do the deliveries, but then come ten o'clock in the morning she would have to leave. 'I've got to go and do my husband's dinner, I've got a family to keep, I've got my own business to run.' And she didn't really want to do the Sunday markets, because she liked to spend Sundays with her husband. Sam would do the early market but then she'd come back and dump the van so she could go down the pub for lunch. And I'd get back from my market and unload her van as well as my own one, while she was having her Sunday dinner. I realise now she was working hard and trying to do right by everyone. But little things like that started to build up, and I started to feel resentful.

In the meantime, Barry had started helping out. And he started pointing things out. Like, at three o'clock in the morning, I was in the shop, and he was in the shop, but where was Sam?

Things got worse. Sam had some really big problems through that time with her own family. She had to prioritise looking after them, but that meant she had less and less time for the Giggly Pig. And everywhere I was going I was hearing, 'Oh, the Giggly Pig! Doesn't Sam Clark own that?' What about me? It was my heart and soul poured into the Giggly Pig, my arse on the line. So that started to grate on me too.

One particular day in the November after I got out, 2007, we were doing a Guy Fawkes thing down at the beach at Shoeburyness, for the Round Table. And we needed to buy some lights, because it was an evening thing. I walked into a shop in Harold Hill, and the bloke behind the desk said, 'Oh, Giggly Pig, oh yeah, Sam and Phil Clark own that.'

I lost it. 'No, they don't own the Giggly Pig, I own the Giggly Pig and I don't know where you got that from.'

I got back in the van, and I was fuming. I rang her up. Before I got the chance to say anything, she started on me.

'One of your pigs has just got out on the M25.'

I said, 'Don't be so ridiculous.' If they had got out on the M25, there would have been massive carnage. I knew there was no way they could have.

'Oh, well, it nearly did, but the bloke driving into the yard shooed it back in.'

'No way, that did not happen.'

'It did happen – that's what the bloke said to me, and now Phil is going mad.'Blah, blah, blah.

And I could hear Phil shouting and swearing in the background,'Pig on the M25. Fucking pig on the M25.'

That was it. I said,'I tell you what, I'm absolutely sick to death of you, I don't want to be your partner anymore.'

'Right then. Well, you'd better get your pigs off my land then.'

'Fine.'

That was the end of my relationship with Sam. The best and longest friendship of my life.

When we'd both calmed down we spoke again, and she said obviously I didn't have to get the pigs off straight away. Which was good of her. But it was frosty. We weren't mates anymore. And the atmosphere when I had to go on her land to tend to the pigs was terrible. She and Phil gave me six months to get the pigs off.

Me and Barry found a piece of land and then it was a big rush, to sort the lease, get it cleared, build the piggery, insulate the roof, fence it off, so we could get the pigs there. And obviously, start of a new business, we didn't have any money. Everything we earned was going into paying builders, every week we had to somehow find the next lot of money.

The day in May we came to get the pigs off her land, me and Sam had another really nasty row, nearly came to blows. And I haven't spoken to her since.

The next drama was over planning permission for my mobile home. When we found the land we knew we'd have to live on it too, and I put in a planning application for a mobile home. I paid an agent £1000 to do it for me, but I got it refused. I actually cried over that one. But I picked myself up, and wrote another planning application myself. If you'd asked me, I would have said I couldn't do it, but I had to do it, so I did. I set out all the reasons why I needed to live on site – the pigs were going to be farrowing through the night, the farm backed onto a housing estate and kids might try to get in. I put in all about my NVQs. And I went up to the planning centre and I was this crazy bird who wanted to do pig farming and really I wasn't going to go away until they'd said yes. The application went through in May 2008, just before we were due to move onto the site. I was elated.

I quickly came to hate that dirty tin can of a mobile home. It was like an oven in the summer and a freezing hellhole in the winter. There was no bath at the end of a day of slog in the cold. There was no wardrobe – my clothes were all hung on the backs of doors. One time the pipes froze and there was no hot water at all, I had to go to Mum's to wash. And it meant I could never get away from it, I was there 24/7.

But when I won that planning permission, it was one of the happiest times. I really felt like I'd achieved something, and it was a huge weight off my mind.

Alongside all the hard work, and the dramas, and the grief, something good was happening – though I didn't realise it at first. A few months after I came out of prison, Mum saw something in the *Sun* newspaper about the Trading Places award for people who had turned their lives around by running their own business. She rung up for an application form for me, and then she nagged me and nagged me about filling it in. Finally, when it was a week before the deadline, I found the time to fill it in. A month later, they rang and said what a brilliant story it was. Another couple of months and they rang to say I was in the top fifty. Then top twenty-five. Then in September 2007, they rang and said I was in the top ten. They came and did some filming of me, with the pigs in the fields at about five o'clock in the morning. And then in October it was the awards ceremony, at the Grosvenor Hotel in London.

Stella drove me up to London. After I got out of prison, we had got back in touch again and now she would always offer to help out if she could. Warren was dead, and Stella hadn't spoken to her daughter Denise for years. I was shocked at first to see the change in Stella. She'd lost her house and was living in a one-bedroom council flat, waiting to have an operation on her legs. But she was still Stella. She still always had a crowd around her, she had a wealthy benefactor who liked a game of Monopoly on a Friday night, and her disability car was top of the range.

I had four tickets for the ceremony and I took Barry, and I took Paul, who'd lent me the money, and I took my mum. This was right when things were turning sour with Sam, and I did put Sam's nose out of joint by not taking her. I think from then on she was spoiling for a fight with me.

It was the best day of my life. We got there early, and we all got ready together in my room. Before the ceremony there was some press there doing photos, and then we all sat round big tables for a dinner. I got really drunk because the drink was all free. After dinner, they started the awards ceremony. Fiona Bruce was hosting it, and she showed the films they had made of all the nominees. When it came to my one, I did think it was quite good and I was in with a chance. Then it all happened really quickly. They said I'd won and I went up onto the stage, and there were three hundred people in the room all giving me a standing ovation. It was brilliant. I made a speech, and they gave me a bowl, and a huge plaque, and a big cheque, which I lost that evening because I was so drunk. I was invited for more drinks but they had to take me back to my room because I was just overwhelmed with it all. There was a big drama the next day when I found out I'd lost all my awards, but someone had found them and they'd been put in a safe for me.

That award did a lot for me; it catapulted me out there.

The papers couldn't get enough of me, and the radio and TV. I started winning other awards, for the quality of the sausage. We won five golds at the British Pig Executive Awards 2008. My name and my story were getting out.

The money I won meant I could get some stability into my business too. The shop where we made the sausages was owned by Len the butcher. He looked like a cuddly lovely old man, and he liked to make out he was stupid, but he wasn't.

Len had always said to me, from the start, 'It's all well and good, darling, but I don't know how long it's gonna last. I'm gonna sell the shop and they're going to turn it into an Indian takeaway.' He had to, because he needed the money. That was hanging over me, because if Len sold the shop I'd have no premises. Winning the Trading Places award meant I could buy Len out and pay him to work for me. OK, I ended up paying £600 to have the premises deep-cleaned. And OK, my employee was old and knackered. But it was a start.

But the worst grief of all was nothing to do with the business.

In March 2008 I found out I was pregnant. Forty-three and I got pregnant just like that – I couldn't believe it! We were about to move the pigs off Sam's land and onto ours, I was applying for planning permission for a mobile home – it was all going on. This put a bit of a spanner in the works, but a nice spanner.

I started to put plans in place about how the business was going to run when the baby came. I was going to have to take a step back from the shop and the farm, and my mum was going to stop working and look after the baby when I went to markets at the weekend. We'd need a bigger mobile home too.

I remember walking around Mothercare when I was about nineteen weeks pregnant, and I was tempted to buy some bits but something stopped me. In September, Mum came with me for my second scan, the twenty-week scan, where you can find out whether it's a girl or a boy. I didn't want to find out but I let them tell my mum. Everything was fine.

I started feeling ill on the way home. Flu-ey. I laid on Mum's settee all day and it got worse. Barry came round and I said I couldn't go back home with him; I wanted to stay there, I didn't feel well. After he went, the pain kept getting worse, and I was screaming for my mum, and she had to get an ambulance. At A&E they said it was just normal pregnancy pain. I knew it wasn't normal pregnancy pain. Then they examined me and said I was dilated. I'd been in labour all day. They said, 'What's going to happen is, you're going to have the baby.' Barry was there by then, and he asked them: was the baby going to live? No, they said, because it was only twenty-one, twenty-two weeks. There was nothing they could do.

Another two weeks and the baby could have lived.

It all happened very quickly. I had some gas and air and she was born three hours later – she just flew out. They let me have her with me for the whole day; I held her for the whole day. I had photos taken, and the chaplain came in. And then they took her away.

Afterwards, they said that I had been leaking fluid for a day but not realised it. If I had known in time, I could have gone and had a stitch put in, but I didn't know, I didn't realise. There was no reason why it happened, they said. No answers.

I do feel that losing my baby Louie was a punishment. Payback. 'You got rid of all them babies, and this will teach you a lesson now.' When I delivered her and held her in my arms, dead at twenty-two weeks, she was only four weeks older than that unnamed baby I'd aborted more than twenty years earlier.

I went to bed for a fortnight. I couldn't face anyone or anything, the pain was unbelievable. I wanted to scream with it, howl with the pain and the grief. They put me back on my antidepressants. Then we had a funeral, a proper funeral.

Time helps. But I don't think I'll ever get over it really. I've still got the photos and her ashes, but I don't look at the photos anymore, and I've put the ashes away because it hurts too much, looking at them. And there's a customer at one of the markets who was pregnant the same time as me, and I look at her with her twins every Sunday and think: my baby would be that old now.

I threw myself into the business in 2009. By the end of the year, I was ready to go to the next level. I'd paid Paul back, built the new piggery, bought the shop off Len. I was ready to grow, to go on to bigger and better things.

Barry was working for me full-time by then. He was my right-hand man, and Mum was helping out (with the two of them not speaking to each other) and I had Len, but I needed more help. I gradually took on all the others – Steve, another cantankerous old butcher; Brian, the local butcher everyone used to get their bags of meat off for barbecues, doing one day a week for me at first but now full-time – he don't cause me any problems; Brian's friend Steve (a different Steve) and this bloke Barry (a different Barry) who both do one day a week for me making sausage; and little Joe, who I took on as a favour to his dad to keep him out of the clubs in Croydon, but he knows his stuff. That's the butchers and the sausage-makers.

Then I took on Scott, who worked on the farm with the pigs and the vans and the equipment. And then his girlfriend Shell, Wesley, Lee, Scrumpy Jack, Becky, Jan, James, Heidi, Leanne, Joan, and Brian's daughters Joanne and Lindsey. They pack the sausages for me, or sell them at the markets. Some of them work full-time for me, some of them just do a Sunday market to earn a little bit of money.

And last year, we could afford to take on someone to clean the pigs out, which meant me and Barry didn't have to do that anymore when we got back from the markets. That was killing me – I really thought I might have a heart attack with the stress of it all.

At one point it looked like the prison farm might shut down and I joked that Mr and Mrs Coveney could come and work for me. That would have been lovely because I would have had people I could completely rely on.

As it is, the lot of them are all misfits, all struggling with life – there's some really sad stories. And they're all busy back-stabbing and tittle-tattling and breaking things. It's like you've taken the cast of *Shameless* and put them all to work in a pig-farming business in Romford. There's good things about all of them I suppose. I just don't know what they are.

I prefer working with immigrants. Usually they're trying to learn the trade as quick as they can, so they can go and make something of themselves back home. So they work hard, they don't complain, they do what you ask them to do – they're prepared to go that extra mile. And I like that they're focused, they've got goals, they're doing something con-structive with their money. Once they've learnt to speak English they're the ones I trust to run the shop when I'm not there – John and Janny. And Paul's in charge of the pigs now. He didn't know anything about pigs when he got here – I had to teach him everything – but he could knock up a nice Romanian salad.

Most of my workers, wherever they've come from, have run-ins with my mum. There's always issues, always dramas. When I'm not there, she thinks she's in charge, and she ter-rorises them. Terrorises them and moans about everything.

Every so often I have a run-in with her too and I get so cross I sack her, but then it's the tears and the tantrums and the not speaking and I have to have her back. She's sixty-nine – she doesn't need to be packing sausages at her age. Honestly, I'd rather pay her to not work there, the amount of arguments she causes. I'd rather she didn't work, and she was just my mum, looking after my Jack Russells and cooking me a roast dinner every now and then.

Don't get me wrong – I do love my mum very much. And I do know I'm lucky she's stood by me all through my life: she's always been there for me, 100 per cent. She's putting me through it a bit now but I suppose I've put her through more than what most daughters put their mothers through, so I just have to put up with it.

The staff have made life easier, because there's no way I could do it all myself anymore. But they've made life harder too because I never know what problem they're going to throw at me next and because I've had to take on a lot of their problems. If someone has a personal problem that means they can't come to work, or they're at work but no good to me, I need to sort it. That's the hardest thing now – finding the staff. I think it's everywhere; Mr Tesco must get it as well.

So now, six years of pure slog after I broke them pigs out of prison, here I am.

It's hard. It's full-on. There's never a day off. When you're meant to get a day off, you don't really get a day off. It's just constant, no let-up. I buy my Sunday papers and they don't get read until Tuesday. Years ago, I would never go out on a

Sunday without reading the papers. Eat, sleep, Giggly Pig, that's my life. 24/7. There are still days, to be honest, when I'm knackered and worn out, and I think, What am I doing?

It is getting easier. I don't do everything myself anymore.

But I still take all the bookings, for markets and hog roasts and festivals. I still do all the paperwork and the accounts. I'm the one working out how much sausage in what flavours we need every week, and how many pigs we have to send to slaughter, and how many pigs we have to be breeding now, and how much feed we need. And who's going to go to what market and what hog roast, and what equipment they all need. Whenever anything goes wrong, I'm the one they ring. My phone doesn't stop. I've got two phones and neither of them ever stop. I wish I could be like Dolly the sheep and clone myself, but I can't.

What's kept me going is the pigs. I have to keep going for them. And I still love them. Especially the saddlebacks. They're lovely pigs, mellow, and gentle, really good mums. Most of them, I don't get too close to, because I know how it ends, but some of them I can't help it.

And I do love being my own boss and being the one who makes the decisions. In prison, that privilege is often taken from you.

And the business just keeps growing. Started off with thirty pigs, one van, six flavours, thirty runs of sausage a week and nowhere to sell from. Now I've got seven hundred pigs, twelve vans, five hog roast machines, a shop, seventy-five flavours, probably three hundred runs a week. I do about fifty farmers' markets, I do food festivals, and I do hog roasts. I can barely keep up with demand. It's mad. I love it.

When I think of what I've achieved in six years, it's amazing, and I'm proud.

And I know everyone who used to be ashamed of me, and
disappointed in me, is proud of me now too. My dad, who
knows how hard it is to make a living this way. My mum – I
can start to redeem myself now for all that trouble I put her
through. Stella's proud of me. Old friends are proud of me.
People who buy sausage from me. Even my old teachers, and
people who never liked me.

And I do lots of talks, one a week at least. In prisons, or for
the Women's Institute, or at churches for old folk. Tell my
story, sell some sausage. My mum never comes, which hurts
a bit. I know she is proud of me, but she finds it difficult to
show it.

And the radio and TV are always after me. I've been on
Farming Today, *You and Yours*, *Countryfile* twice. *Countryfile* is
a big thing, it has 10 million viewers, everyone watches
Countryfile. You know you've made it when you've been on
Countryfile, you've arrived. There's a lot of farmers that have
never been on *Countryfile* and I've not done it once, I've done
it twice.

The first time I was on *Farming Today*, I wanted Dad to
know about it. He'd come to visit me a couple of times in
prison, and he'd come to my party when I got out of prison,
but I hadn't really seen him since. I couldn't ring him because
it was very difficult between me and his new wife, Jean, so I
found the number for a friend of his called John Smith and
left a message: can you tell Doug Mackness his daughter
Tracy's going to be on *Farming Today*. John Smith was a
former county councillor who owned a lot of land out near

Stansted and he and my dad farmed it: the rogue and the gentleman. Later that day, John Smith rang me back and left a message to say they'd both listened to it, the pair of them sitting out in a field on their tractors. He said my dad had been very proud of me, he'd actually had a tear welling up in his eye.

The best was, I went back to visit the prison last year, and the Governor, Mr Carruthers, came running out to greet me. He was so proud of me. He'd seen me on the telly, and he'd seen me in the papers, and they'd put the picture of me from the papers up in the central office, the hub of the whole prison. They all big me up there, and when a new girl comes, they say listen, you can do this, because look at what this other girl done, what Tracy Mackness done. She was there, and she's got her own business now, and she's been on telly and in the papers. I'm quite famous in all the prisons for it.

I'm more on the manor now than I ever was. But instead of people fearing me or hating me, people respect me, I am accepted, I get pats on the back. Everyone round here knows who I am, everybody has heard of the Giggly Pig, and I like that.

20

LEARNING FROM THE PAST, DREAMING OF THE FUTURE

I've certainly had plenty of time, in prison, to think about my life – what I've done, and where I've gone wrong, and what I've learnt from my mistakes. What I regret, and which bits I don't regret, even though you might think I would. And my plans and dreams for the future.

So, what went wrong?

I do regret not staying on at school and taking my exams. If I could change one thing, that would be it. I'm not stupid; if I'd stayed on at school, I could probably have done any-thing. Maybe gone to college or university, maybe become a lawyer or something like that. Some kind of career where you know where your pound notes are coming from and that the bills are going to be paid. When I look at families now, and how they nurture their kids, help them take the right direction, I do feel a bit let down, a bit like I should have been getting some better guidance, not just left to my own devices, left to fend for myself. I don't blame my teachers. I wasn't there, so there wasn't anything they could do. But I do think my family could have given me better guidance.

And I do wish my mum hadn't divorced my dad. Because she does admit now that really he was probably the best person she was ever with. She's never had anyone since who's been as good. And my dad felt so bad about the divorce that we didn't see much of him after that. He had his new bird Jean, and his new kids, and he started a new life. The family unit was just busted up, and the job I always thought I was going to do – working on the stall and in the shop – I couldn't do. I suppose you could say that if he hadn't gone to prison Mum wouldn't have divorced him but then where does that end?

Then the other two things that were my downfall were my tastes for money and men.

I've always liked the pound note. Always had champagne tastes and beer man's money, always wanted the more expensive version, always lived beyond my means. Even when I had a job, I always had more outgoings than incomings because I couldn't ever settle for second best and I wanted it now. When I was fifteen, I remember writing a list of things I always wanted and it was a TR7 car, going to Barbados, a nice watch, a house by the river. And I was prepared to do whatever I needed to do to get it. Whether that meant not going out for a few weeks so I could have the curtains I wanted, or selling some speed so I could have the flat

I wanted, as far as I was concerned I was doing what I had to do to get what I wanted. Weird. I'm not like it now.

Obviously, I've made very bad choices with men. I don't know what it is – the excitement, I think. Mum is always asking me, why can't you just have a boyfriend with a normal job, nine to five? But for me it's too boring. They drive me insane. I've tried it, and I've got nothing in common with them. I need someone who's a stronger character than me, who I can respect. If I can't look up to a man, if I don't think he's got balls, he doesn't stand a chance in hell. But then those characters seem to be not very nice.

That's what went wrong. What went right? Not a lot. But enough. What went right, really, was me getting that long sentence. The first sentence I got didn't do me any good – it was too short for me to do anything constructive. I had the wrong attitude because I went in there hating the world, and really it just taught me new ways to do naughty things. It wasn't a deterrent at all.

But the second one was different. That sentence took me from the depths of despair – hating myself, feeling completely worthless – to running my own business. That ten-year stretch gave me the time to think about my life and see what was really going on. And the motivation never to go back there again – a big sentence like that is a deterrent, no doubt about that. And the opportunities to do something about it. To get myself educated, and to learn a trade.

Prison gave me the opportunity to channel my energy into something positive – without any distractions. I've always done whatever I do to the best of my ability, but unfortunately what I've done hasn't always been the right things. Once, I partied and scammed and sold cocaine to the best of my ability. Now I sell sausages. I always got a buzz out of taking risks. Once, it was shoplifting and running drug money. Now I get my buzz from taking risks with the business – taking on more and more markets and festivals and seeing if I can meet the demand. Running the business right on the edge, stretching myself to the limit.

Prison taught me to deal with problems too. My mantra that I learnt in prison still comes in useful –'Deal with it, deal with it.'Before, when things went wrong, I couldn't deal with it, or not constructively. Now I can.

And it helped me to become less impulsive – to take more precautions before I make rash decisions, to look at the bigger picture. Back when I was younger, I was up to all sorts and nothing bothered me, nothing phased me, I couldn't give a shit. My attitude was 'What's the worst they're gonna do, kill me?' Now, I'm the biggest worrier in the world; I get stressed about anything.

So, no, I don't regret prison. In some ways it is probably the best thing that has ever happened to me. In fact, apart from not staying on at school, and having those abortions when I was young – I deeply regret that, not just because I shouldn't have done it but because I think it didn't do me any favours later when I wanted to keep my baby – I can't really say I regret any of it. Because I had to get it all out of my system. And because somehow, it has got me to where I am. And every step of the way I've been learning things, gaining knowledge and experience and skills that help me now. Even working with drug dealers and gangsters, I was honing my negotiation skills, and my bullshit detection skills, and learning how to be one step ahead of some of the most cunning people there are.

I think I was always destined to be a pig farmer. I think everything happened at the right time for the right reasons – all the opportunities were put my way. Even being there that night when I got nicked. Because I needed a long sentence, but I didn't need twenty-five years.

I was always going to end up here, I really do believe that. I think there was a plan for me. I just had to take the long route round for some reason.

But, having said that, the advice I'd give to young people now, knowing what I do, is this. We all think that we know everything. We don't. Don't go down the avenue I went down. Don't waste yourself and waste your life on people that are not worth wasting it on. Drugs are for mugs. Crime definitely doesn't pay. Not in the end. Not when you think about how you have to live, always on the edge, always waiting for the door to be kicked in, always looking in your car mirrors. Now I don't even think about looking in my mirrors unless I'm reversing. And not when you think about what suffering you're going to have to go through when you get caught and go to prison, and what suffering you're going to put your family through. Don't just think about yourself, think about the people you care about, and what effect your actions are going to have on them. Think about the suffering you're going to put your mum through. My mum screamed in court when I got sent down, and that sound will haunt me forever. Think about what suffering you're going to put your children through, being brought up with no mum there or no dad there, crying when they visit you once a week. All for what?

And my advice to people in prison? Prison is a saving grace. If you really want to turn your life around, you can do it in prison. There's everything there to help you. There's the officers for advice, there's the courses, there's the time to think. If you want it, you can make it happen. So use your time. Think about your future. Start planning now. Work, learn, make prison work for you, so that you can change your life. A lot of people say they're going to do it, but hardly any actually manage it.

I hope my success story will help show other people how not to take the wrong path. And I hope it will show that, even if you do take the wrong path, you can still get back on the right one. No matter how low you are, you can always get back on top. My story shows it can be done.

My own future – I don't know what it holds. But I've got lots of plans. Because this ain't it. Where I am, it's not complete, it's not finished.

I'm forty-eight now.

Barry and me, we've been through some tough times; we've split up a couple of times. It isn't easy living with someone and working with them too. But we're still here trying to make it work. Sometimes I think I would like to have met someone who could have looked after me and taken care of me all my life, so I didn't have to worry every day about making it happen. But I've never had that. Except maybe with Chopper's Charlie. And then I think: I wouldn't want to be one of them that always has to be asking, 'Can I have this, can I have that?' I like to have my own money, I like to do what I want to do. So I don't know if that ever could have been the life for me.

Children – I did always think I would have children. But there was no question with Mitchell Binnington, my first husband, or with Frankie Farrell down in Wickford, and Warren Walker, who I did want a baby with, had had a vasectomy. And even when I was thirty-six, thirty-seven, I was still thinking I had plenty of time. Then I got nicked and resigned myself to the fact I wasn't going to have any. I couldn't believe it when I got pregnant straight away with Barry. And then I lost her.

Mum still goes on at me about babies. She won't let it go; she's like a dog with a bone. She's always telling me about women who have had IVF in Barcelona at forty-seven, or asking people in the shop if they'll donate some sperm (she's joking, but she's not). I do think about IVF, maybe with someone else's eggs. And I think about adoption. I know I've got a really bad record and been in prison, but that doesn't make me a bad person, and I've never done anything to children. I've got money, I've got a nice environment.

But I don't know. Maybe I'm too old. How would I cope with all the hopes and disappointments of IVF? I don't think I could cope with any more disappointments, any more knock-backs. How would I cope with a child and run the business? Mum always says she would look after a baby, but the fuss she makes about having my dogs, I doubt it.

Maybe it's better to forget about children and move on.

I think I'm going to have to be happy with what I've got. Try to think about the positive things about not having children, and be content with my dogs. My four Jack Russells, Sausage, Mash, Gravy and Chops. They give me as much trouble as children. And I think I love them as much, and they love me. I cook them chickens to eat every day, I take care of them, I worry about who's going to look after them when I'm not there. When I went away and left them with Mum for three weeks, I didn't have any way of telling them I was coming back. When I walked through the door, they were so excited they all wet themselves.

I do get lonely sometimes because I don't really have mates now. I have associates, people I work with, that I can go down the bingo with. But not friends, people I could tell my secrets to, people I could back-stab a bloke to. Stella and Sam were my friends. Loyal friends, good friends, they did a lot for me and I did a lot for them. Now Stella and me haven't got much in common anymore. We still help each other out – she might go to the cash and carry for me, and I might bung her £50 and a load of free sausages. But the days of what we used to do are gone.

And Sam and me don't speak. There wasn't a day I didn't speak to her, and now we don't speak at all – four years we haven't spoken. Phil said it would end in tears if we went into business together and I remember those words every day.

But I can't go back to going out and about, and to dealing with all the dramas of other people's lives, I've got enough to contend with here. And I do know that if I really had a problem, a really big one, Stella would still be there for me, and even probably Sam wouldn't turn me away from her door. I know that I've got people if I'm in real trouble.

Longer term, I need to get the business to the point where I don't have to work as hard as I am now. I know I can't work like this forever. I'm forty-eight now, and in seven years' time, when I'm fifty-five, I'm certainly not going to be doing this. After fifty-five, I'm not going to be able to lift and carry and shout and scream and worry and graft like I do now. It's a killer.

So I've got all kinds of plans. Maybe I'll sell out to a supermarket or a bigger business. Maybe I'll give the business to my brother and he can run it for me and give me a set amount of money each week. Then he gets a good wage and I get a good wage. He can't do block paving for much longer. In the meantime, I want to build it, do more and more with it. I've always wanted my own sausage and mash cafe, so maybe I'll do that.

Plus, I've got my two properties, my flat and my house, that I rent out at the moment. Somehow, through everything, I've managed to hang on to them. They're remortgaged, to pay my confiscation orders, so I have to rent them out, but in ten years' time I'll have paid them off. And what I earn now, I save for my pension, I don't spend. I don't buy clothes, I don't go out. I've got a little Peugeot that I've had since when I was in prison; I live in a mobile home.

So, what I want to do, is work like a dog for the next seven years. Work hard now, kill myself now, keep growing the business. And then, ten years' time, I'd like to be somewhere warm taking it easy and not worrying. Me, and maybe Barry if we can stick each other that long, and my dogs.

I still got lots more ambitions. I'm never going to stand still. Like I said to Mr Carruthers, my old Governor, the day I left prison: 'Look out, you definitely ain't seen the last of me.'

ACKNOWLEDGEMENTS

I would like to thank Simon & Schuster and my brilliant editor Kerri Sharp, who loved this book from the beginning. I also want to thank my agent Andrew Lownie, and Deborah Crewe – without her, this book would not have been written.

I want to thank my Mum, who has been there from Day One. Thanks to Stella and Sam for the good times. I am grateful to Mr Carruthers, the prison governor, who must have seen something in me, and Lorraine Coveney, who made me believe in myself. If it wasn't for Paul (Alfie), I could never have set my business up, and if it wasn't for Barry, I could never have kept it going. Thank you Paul, thank you Barry. Finally, thank you to my gorgeous dogs – Mash, Gravy, Sausage and Chops: you're monsters, but you make me very happy.